OREGON
MOONSHINE

OREGON
MOONSHINE

BOOTLEGGERS, BUSTS & BRAWLS

BRUCE HANEY

AMERICAN PALATE

Published by American Palate
A Division of The History Press
Charleston, SC
www.historypress.com

First published 2023

Manufactured in the United States

ISBN 9781467153027

Library of Congress Control Number: 2022948306

For Rachel

CONTENTS

CONTENTS

ACKNOWLEDGEMENTS

History people are some of the nicest people. I am always pleasantly surprised by how willing people are to help a fellow history researcher, and I am glad that I get the opportunity in each book to thank them, as this project wouldn't be quite what it is without their help.

First, I would like to thank the people who helped me with research on Nettie Connett. Thank you to Alex Trail, who knew Nettie and told me so many great stories. Thank you to Dan Bosserman for sharing articles that he wrote about her. Thank you to Ken Funk for all his help when I was researching at the Sandy History Museum. Thanks to the staff of the Sandy History Museum, as well, for sharing their wonderful photos of Nettie. Also, thank you to Mark Moore of PdxHistory.com, who shared some articles about her that I would never have come across on my own.

I would like to acknowledge The History Press as well. Every person that I have worked with during the creation of my last book, *Eccentric Tales of Boring, Oregon*, was a joy to work with and added to what that book is. Thank you to Hilary Parrish, Sarah Haynes and especially Laurie Krill, who saw my potential and pitched my last book as well as this book.

It was a big challenge to find all the photos I wanted to use in this book. These museums and people were helpful in making it as chock-full of photos as it is: the Lane County Historical Museum, Benton County Historical Society, Columbia County Museum Association, Clackamas County Historical Society and the Umatilla Historical Society. Here is a list of the people from those places that helped me: Stephen O'Brien, Patti

Larkin, Les Watters, Joe Lynn Dow, Sandra McGuire, April Meadows and Virginia Roberts.

In my last book, I forgot to thank David Scheer, so I am doing it here. David, your knowledge of the Independent Order of Odd Fellows was a help in a couple of chapters of that book.

A couple more thank-yous are in order. Every month—well, almost every month—I give a speech about the town of Boring, Oregon, at the Boring Community Planning Organization. I have been doing this for five years now, and I appreciate the platform they give me each month, as I have become a better public speaker, writer and researcher because of it. Lastly, a big thanks to Rachel Rogers, who is always my first reader and picks up the slack when I am working toward a deadline.

INTRODUCTION

When one thinks about Prohibition and moonshiners, Oregon is, of course, the first locale that comes to mind. Actually, most people's minds conjure up images of rough men operating stills in the mountains of Georgia, North Carolina and Tennessee. But Oregon had more than its fair share of moonshiners during Prohibition. With our rain and our trees, we have plenty of places to hide a still and abundant out-of-the-way water sources to use for the distilling process. During my research, I have come across hundreds of moonshiners, and those are just the ones who got caught.

Oregonians were making moonshine well before Prohibition came along—even before Oregon became a state in 1859. Back in 1844, when it was still called the Oregon Territory, James Conner was making, selling and getting in trouble for his moonshine, which he called Blue Ruin.

There were other early moonshiners, as well. There was an interesting character in Baker County named Lum whose operation was busted around 1901, and then there were the McKenzie River Bandits, who started their distillery around 1912 but stayed one step ahead of the law until their first bust in 1915.

The year 1916 is when moonshining took off and became many people's side hustle in the Beaver State. The reason is that Oregon went dry that year. Oregon had been slowly becoming a dry state since 1904. That was the year that Oregon voted on the Local Option Act, which allowed jurisdictions to vote on their community being wet or dry. In 1905, Hood River became the first dry town. In 1907, Clackamas County went dry.

Though it was still legal to distill in most of Oregon in 1910, doing it without paying for licenses and taxes could get you thrown in jail. That is why, in 1910, United States revenue agents were scouring Oregon looking for moonshiners. L.F McPherson, an old Oregonian, was busted for making prune brandy during these searches. It was rumored that he had been operating for three years.

In 1913, Hillsboro and Milwaukie went dry. Salem voted that way as well that year, but the vote was challenged, and they didn't go completely dry until 1914.

In 1915, the Anderson Act was passed; it went into effect on January 1, 1916. The law made it illegal to sell, barter or make intoxicating liquor. There were a few exceptions written into the law. It was legal for alcohol to be used for medical, mechanical, scientific or sacramental purposes. With this act becoming law, it wasn't long before moonshining and bootlegging became a big business.

Ben Jarrell, a man from North Carolina who had a bit of debt to pay off, traveled to Oregon that year because it was so profitable to make and sell moonshine in the now-dry state of Oregon. North Carolina was dry as well, but there were already many moonshiners filling the void there. Out here, he was able to earn enough to pay off his debt, though he did land in jail a few times during the process.

Officers in front of confiscated distilling equipment from various raids. *Courtesy of Columbia County Museum Association.*

Officers with captured barrels and a small still. *Courtesy of Deschutes County Historical Society.*

Oregon is full of moonshine stories, and the ones mentioned here are just a small taste of the tales I have found for you. Just like the stories from the South, Oregon has moonshiners involved in car chases, hidden operations, shootouts and even an attempted murder involving dynamite. This book is not meant to be a history of Prohibition, though I give some facts about it throughout, for context. The purpose of this book is to tell the story of how Prohibition affected Oregon and Oregonians and to document all the interesting events that happened in this state because of it.

Moonshine even affected this Oregonian, as well. Here is my story. I always wanted to try moonshine, because I liked its outlaw spirit. So, I would mention this to people all the time, whenever someone was telling a drinking story.

One time, this person I was talking to, a person I didn't even know, said that he had a little bottle of moonshine, and he gave it to me. He was a stranger, but I took it, because I had always wanted to try it. I didn't drink it at that moment. It was a small bottle, but it had probably four good shots of alcohol in it. I decided to save it for a get-together at my friend's house, and I made a big deal about it: "Hey, I have real moonshine." So, I poured the four shots. Three for my friends and one for myself. But one of my friends didn't drink hard liquor or possibly had reservations about putting some strange,

Photo from a postcard showing five sheriffs sitting on bottles of seized rum. *Courtesy of Stephen Kenny.*

clear, unregulated alcohol that I obtained from a stranger into her body. So, I took her shot, as well. The next morning, I woke up with little memory of the night before, and I had to get the story from my friends. Apparently, I was dancing and singing along to that '90s hit from Right Said Fred, "I'm Too Sexy." The thing is, I am not sexy, let alone "too" sexy; I don't know how to dance; and I hate that song. That was the first and last time that I ever indulged in moonshine.

This book is in chronological order, for the most part, but I wrote it in the tradition of a great collection of short stories, so that the tales can be read and enjoyed in any order the reader chooses. So, if you're reading this and saw in the table of contents that a chapter has a title with your hometown or county in it, feel free to jump to that one and read it, or if you see is a subject that piques your interest, read about that first. No judgment. The book won't be ruined if you read "Tusko's Ten-Gallon Toddy" before you read "McKenzie River Bandits." I get it. It would be hard for me not to skip right to the story about an elephant being given ten gallons of moonshine. Those are the types of stories from history that fascinate me, and it's what I enjoy researching and writing about. I am always looking for a good story, and I believe I have found quite a few exciting and interesting moonshine tales for you. Enjoy.

PART I

PIONEER MOONSHINERS

CHAPTER 1

MOONSHINERS IN THE OREGON TERRITORY

E ven before Oregon was a state, there were people getting in trouble for making liquor. One of the first was James Conner.

James Conner was described as a mountain man by Henry Spalding, a Presbyterian mission leader. Spalding met Conner in 1836 when Spalding hired him and a few other mountain men in Daniel, Wyoming, for a mission he was leading to the Pacific Northwest. Spalding was worried about the character of these men. In the book by Clifford Drury simply titled *Henry Harmon Spalding*, it is written that Spalding was "fearful that the mountain men, unsympathetic to missionaries, might cause trouble by influencing the Indians to make exorbitant demands."

After spending time with the missionaries, Conner joined their congregation. On December 23, 1838, Conner stood up and spoke during a sermon, telling the congregation how he had lived a wicked life and that he wished to change. In 1839, he was baptized. Later, Spalding spoke of Conner with high regard, saying, "He has been lawfully married to a Nez Perce woman, speaks the language well, and judging from his work so far this fall, will be of great service to me."

But the love for Conner from the Presbyterians would not last. In February 1843, after the church had made its way to Oregon, Conner was suspended. The notes in the church's minutes book state the reason as "the sin of Sabbath Breaking, neglect of religious duties and fighting." Spalding himself added a note to the book later that read, "It has since proven that he has been guilty of polygamy, sending a challenge to fight a duel, and vending liquor."

Left: A photograph of Henry Spalding, believed to be circa 1850. *Courtesy of the archives of the Pacific University, Oregon.*

Below: Here you can see a good example of the "worm"; it is the coiled bit of copper in the center of the photo. *Courtesy of Deschutes County Historical Society.*

Opposite: Two people canoeing on the Columbia River. *Courtesy of the Library of Congress.*

In Oregon City, Conner got himself into the liquor business by buying some materials from the Abernethy store. He used sheer-tin pipes in a primitive zigzag pattern for the worm and a wooden through to distill the alcohol. The worm is a coil that is submerged in water and acts as a condenser, taking the alcohol vapors and turning them into a liquid.

The man who busted Conner was Dr. Elijah White, a United States sub-Indian agent and Methodist missionary. The Methodists already had a history in the Oregon Territory of being Prohibition-minded. In 1936, Methodist missionaries formed the Oregon Temperance Society.

Elijah White was born in 1806 in Bath, New York. He lived the early part of his life there, where he was educated at a school of medicine and married a woman named Sarepta. They had two children by the time they moved to Oregon, one of whom was adopted.

Oregon would be a tragic place for the family. The first tragedy took place in 1838, when Sarepta was traveling in a canoe with their infant son, Jason, on the Columbia River. During their journey, the canoe flipped over, and Jason drowned. Their adopted son died the next year while trying to cross the Willamette River on horseback.

Elijah White received word in January 1844 that there was a liquor operation in Oregon City. White had no real authority in this matter, but he believed the laws of Iowa that covered making and selling liquor in Indian

Willamette Falls, near Portland, Ore.

Above: Willamette Falls.
Author's collection.

Right: Hiram Straight
Jr. served two terms as
mayor of Oregon City.
*Courtesy of the Clackamas
County Historical Society.*

territory could be applied, since this was Indian territory and he was a sub-Indian agent for the federal government.

James Conner's DIY distillery was seized and destroyed. For operating this still, Conner was held on a $300 bond. This charge had no grounds, since there was no law against operating a still at the time, but that didn't stop the legislature from collecting the $300.

This setback didn't hold back Conner for very long. When summer came around, he was operating a new still with two other men. One was Richard McCrary, a trapper. The other was Hiram Straight.

Hiram Straight and his family had arrived in Oregon the previous year via the Oregon Trail. After working with James Conner, Straight would enter politics. In 1846, he served in the Provisional Legislature of Oregon. Straight was nervous about appearances when he entered politics, because he had no coat and he thought he would look silly in just a striped shirt. Luckily for him, a friend named Sidney Moss sold him a tailored coat for forty dollars in scrip. In 1894, his son, Hiram Straight Jr., would become mayor of Oregon City.

Conner, McCrary and Straight's still was a step up from the last one. This time, it was made with a large kettle, a wooden top and a proper worm. The liquor that they made was from wheat, molasses and shorts, and it was nicknamed Blue Ruin. The "blue" in the name most likely has nothing to do with the color. The term *blue ruin* had been around for many years before this. In the 1811 *Dictionary of the Vulgar Tongue* by Francis Grose, *blue ruin* is defined simply as "Gin. Blue Ribband; gin." *Ribband* is another term for ribbon. So, by using that phrase, the men were probably either implying that it was either a "blue ribbon"–quality product or saying that when it comes to ruining a person, this product gets the blue ribbon.

Elijah White was quick to bust this still, as well. Conner, furious at White, challenged him to a duel. This was a much bigger offense than the liquor making.

White did not take him up on the dual; instead, he beat him with the law. This time, Conner was hit with a $500 fine and was disenfranchised for life. Mostly, this meant that he lost his right to vote.

Later that year, the disenfranchisement was remitted in an act titled "For the Relief of James Conner," in which it was written that "1844, against James Conner be and the same is hereby remitted; and that all the disabilities flowing from the judgment of said court be and the same are hereby removed and that the said James Conner be restored to all the privileges of a citizen of Oregon."

That year, as well, Oregon's provisional government passed a law to "prevent the introduction, sale and distillation of ardent spirits in Oregon." This early prohibition law was repealed in 1849.

The James Conner incident was a minor blip in the history of illegal liquor production in Oregon. It could have been worse; White could have taken Conner up on his challenge, and one of them would have ended up dead, possibly both. This first incident had no bloodshed, but many years later, when the Prohibition Act went into effect, there was much blood spilled in the quest to make a profit making moonshine.

Chapter 2

HALF-TRUTHS AND MOONSHINE ALONG THE SNAKE RIVER

Christopher Columbus Davis lived an interesting life, and depending on which sources you choose to believe, he was either an Old West hero or an outlaw. Legally speaking, he never got in trouble for his actions—that is, until he tried his hand at moonshining. He might have been named after Christopher Columbus, but instead of going by Christopher or even by Columbus, he went by a shortened version of his middle name: he was known as Lum.

Lum was born in 1836 in Greencastle, Indiana. He grew up to be a large man. People described him as both tall and heavy.

Around 1862, when he was in his late twenties, Lum made his way to Oregon. He started out his Oregon life in the area around the Snake River in Baker County, Oregon. Before settling down, he tried other spots in the state. In the winter of that year, he moved to Portland, but he must not have cared for it, because by the summer of '63, he was back in Baker County.

Lum eventually did settle and built his life around mining. He worked in the Rye Valley and Mormon Basin Mines. It was said that while he worked the mines, he carried a Henry rifle over his shoulder in case of Native American attacks. It was also said at the time that Lum was known as a person to go to if you needed someone who could track down a Native American who had taken livestock.

Mining operation near Baker, Oregon. *Author's collection.*

THE SINGLE BULLET INCIDENT

Lum was involved in a famous incident that's been written about in quite a few books on Oregon. The story goes that Lum was searching for a couple of stolen horses and came upon two Native Americans. Lum's version of the story is that they tried to play a game of, in his words, "me good Indian" and then asked if there were other "white men" around. Lum lied and told them there were and pointed away from himself. Both Native Americans turned in the direction he pointed, and when they did, Lum pointed his gun at them and pulled the trigger. According to legend, with this single shot, he killed both men.

This is just one of the stories in Lum's life that have been called to question. In Joseph H. Labadie's book *150 Years of Eastern Oregon History: The Barton-Shumway Family*, the author states that Lum claimed the Native Americans were stealing horses, but it was later proven he was lying.

Another version of the story comes from Gregory Michno's *The Deadliest Indian War in the West*. In this version, it said that Lum and another man were hunting in the area when they came across the two Native Americans. The two men decided to track them. They followed the Native Americans to their camp and caught them when they were just about to cook some meat from a horse they had stolen. How Lum and the other man knew it was a "stolen" horse, we don't know. In this version of the story, the Native Americans tried to flee and were in a line when Lum pointed his Henry rifle at them, then shot and killed them—again, with a single bullet. This version of the story still has the "two Native Americans killed by one bullet" narrative but adds that Lum and the other man wanted to make sure the Native Americans were not playing possum, so they put several more rounds in their limp bodies.

How Lum Found Himself a Wife

The other big story in the life of Lum, of which there are many different versions, is how he came to marry a Chinese woman named Moye. To the local papers, her ethnicity was shocking. When Lum was busted for moonshining, the *Morning Oregonian* ran an article titled "Has a Chinese Wife." From that article, we get the first version of the story:

> *In connection with his Oriental wife, there is quite a romantic story. Davis is an old Indian fighter. He is the product of the half wild border-land civilization. During the Nez Perces Indian war in 1878, the Chinese woman was kidnapped and held for a ransom by a prominent Chinaman while fighting the Indians, so the story goes, Davis "caught on" to the Chinaman's little game, and wrested her from his grasp. She was 13 years old, and rather pretty even to the eye of a white man.*

Different times. In another version of the story, Lum is written as a complete villain; in that version, it is said that he killed a Chinese mining family and stole their gold and their little girl.

The third version of the story goes like this: the girl was kidnapped from Connor Creek, Lum somehow got wind of it, chased down the bad guys and brought Moye back to her parents. Afterward, he ended up marrying her.

The fourth version of the story is also from the *Morning Oregonian* but printed years after Lum's death.

> *About 14 years before that time, it was learned, Davis had first entered the Snake River district. He had made his way to the Snake River by stage to Wild Goose Rapids. On the Stage had been, besides Davis, three wealthy Chinese mining men and a Chinese girl who had been stolen and was being taken to the mining camps for a slave. The party had started across the*

snake river in a boat, when Davis suddenly whipped out a gun and took charge of the situation. On the Oregon side of the river he took the girl and sent the Chinamen back across the river.

Another thing added to some versions is that Lum took the girl to be educated and reared at a Catholic School in Baker City until she was older and then married her.

LUM'S PRUNE MOONSHINE

Whatever the real story was, Moye was still living with Lum nearly twenty years later when he ran into trouble with the law for moonshining. Moye and Lum even had two children together.

Lum's trouble with the law didn't start until 1901, when David Dunn, head of the local revenue office, got a tip that moonshine was showing up in parts of Huntington and Baker City.

Lum had been producing moonshine for a while and had a good system for moving his product. Lum had a talent for playing the violin. He used this talent to get gigs playing at all the local dances. Part of his deal when playing at the dances was that he would bring refreshments. He was always popular at the local dances and made a bit of money doing it.

John W. Minto was the man the revenue office sent to check out Huntington and Baker City for any trace of untaxed liquor. Minto had made many trips without any luck until he ran into a tinner, a tin miner. The tinner told him about a man with the last name Davis who had a distilling operation somewhere up in the mountains.

Minto moved on this tip and made plans to locate the still. To do that, he would need help, so he brought along Deputy Roberts from the United States Marshal's Office for the journey.

Minto and Roberts decided to hire a local driver and team for the trip. They wanted someone who would be familiar with the terrain. Since they were hiring a local, they decided it best not to mention the name of the person they were looking for, in case the driver was a friend of Lum Davis.

The journey took many days, and they checked on many homes without any luck in finding the Davis homestead. While they searched the mountains, they stopped every person they came across and asked about homes in the area. They must have let it slip to one of these people that they were looking for the Davis house, because the driver of the team

People dancing and having a good time in Baker City, Oregon. *Author's collection.*

heard them mention it, and he told Minto and Roberts that he knew exactly where the Davis house was located and that they had been heading in the wrong direction. The driver had no qualms about leading them to Lum Davis, so they turned around and headed back the way they came. They lost much time by keeping this information from the driver, but now they were at least heading in the right direction.

The group made their way through the rugged terrain toward Lum's house. It was located about three miles from the Snake River and a few miles below Huntington. They had almost reached the spot where Lum's house was supposed to be when they came across a man who was coming from the direction of the house. The officers stopped and saluted the man and wished him a pleasant morning before starting to ask him a series of questions. Could this be Mr. Davis, the man they were looking for?

John Minto started the conversation; he got down from the wagon and had a friendly chat with the man. Minto asked him about the area. He asked about mining and farming. Eventually, during the conversation, he was able to figure out that this was the infamous Davis he was talking to. Minto was cautious with his choice of words, because there were rumors that Davis was vocal about his dislike of revenue agents and any form of intruder on his property.

Lum Davis got comfortable enough with Minto that they ended up sitting on the bank together, and Lum drew him a map with little sketches of landmarks in the area. While Lum was drawing the map, Minto casually

Parts of a small still hanging in the Eastern Oregon Museum in Haines, Oregon. *Courtesy of Rachel Rogers.*

reached behind Lum and pulled out the long, well-used bowie knife he had seen protruding from Lum's high-top boot. With Lum's weapon out of the equation, Minto felt comfortable enough to tell Lum that he was under arrest.

At this point, Lum did not resist, but he did shut his mouth as the officers went up to investigate his property. He knew he was caught, but he wasn't going to help them find his still.

The officers started their search around the cabin. It was uncommon but not unheard of for people to have their stills in or around their home, but the search had to start somewhere.

The officers did locate Lum's still away from the house, and they found it to be a well-constructed distillery. It was said that there were whiskey fumes in the area from its use.

Another article told another version of the story, in which the officers found just part of a still and sent that to Portland as evidence. With Lum Davis, the story is never quite clear. Was it part of a still or was it a working still that was found? There's even confusion when it comes to the type of liquor Lum made: the *Sunday Oregonian* spoke of whiskey fumes, but other articles refer to the booze he made as apple and peach brandy. There was even one article that said he made prune brandy. Lum had his own orchards, so he was probably making liquor out of whatever he had a surplus of.

After the officers found what they were looking for, they headed back to the cabin and found that it was full of rifles and ammunition.

What the officers were most shocked about finding at Lum's home was his Chinese wife and what the *Morning Oregonian* referred to as their "half-breed children." After this unpleasant language, the article referred to them as "handsome children."

It was said that Moye and the children were heartbroken to see Lum taken away to Portland for his crimes. There, he was convicted and spent five months in jail and had to pay a fine of $300.

The moonshining incident is the last big story in the life of Christopher Columbus "Lum" Davis, a man who lived a big life of questionable choices that reserved him a spot in the history of Oregon.

CHAPTER 3

McKENZIE RIVER BANDITS

A t ninety miles long, the McKenzie River provided many places to hide a moonshine operation. That is probably one of the leading reasons that the moonshiners operating on it were able to hide their distillery for so long.

It was believed that they had started their moonshine operation in 1910. In 1912, they got close to being caught. Sheriff Bown knew that someone was selling large quantities of liquor to the loggers and other locals. He also believed that it was being made locally. When he was satisfied that his assumption was correct, he brought in revenue agents to assist.

Based on his hunch and research, five revenue officers and two deputy sheriffs went out searching for the moonshiners along the McKenzie River. They were able to locate a dismantled still but found no clues indicating who had built it or who had operated it.

The still was located thirty miles east of Eugene near Leaburg, a town named after Leander Cruzan. Leander was an early resident of the area and the first postmaster. As postmaster, he named the town after himself. In the *Crook County Journal*, it was written that the dismantled still was found under a log, with sacks of cornmeal and barley. Finding the still dismantled would be common with the McKenzie River Bandits. They always seemed to be one step ahead of the law.

Many people must have thought that the captured still would stop the production of moonshine in the area, because the *Sunday Oregonian* wrote: "Now that the moonshine still on the McKenzie has been put out

Old postcard photo of the McKenzie River. *Author's collection.*

of commission, perhaps the fishing stories from that section will be more moderate in the future."

The flow of moonshine continued for another three years. One reason local law enforcement believed that the 'shine was still coming from a local source is that the closer to the area where the distilling was believed to be happening, the cheaper the price was. If you bought moonshine near Leaburg, it was only $1.00 a quart, but thirty miles away in Springfield and Eugene, it went for $1.25 a quart. Moonshine prices fluctuated over the years, especially once Prohibition went into effect.

Sheriff James C. Parker told a reporter, "The people on the McKenzie have been terrorized. They knew where the liquor was coming from, but they feared to tell." This might be true, but no other record of the so-called terrorizing exists outside of statements like these. There were no reports of the moonshiners intimidating or causing injury to any of the locals. It is possible that the locals just wanted to mind their own business or that they didn't want to stop the flow of booze.

Harry Bown, who had been the sheriff since 1906, was replaced by James C. Parker. After that, the McKenzie River Bandits became James Parker's problem. One tactic that got Parker close to catching them was to team up with the district attorney, J.M. Devers. Parker and Devers had the theory that the moonshiners used middlemen to sell the product. Their plan was to

Lane County Sheriff's Office in 1911. Pictured are James C. Parker (*far left*) and Harry L. Bown (*far right*). *Courtesy of the Lane County History Museum.*

buy booze from them and work their way up the chain until they found the ringleaders of the operation.

The two didn't have to work their way as far up the chain as they thought, because it turned out that these moonshiners were peddling the product themselves. Before realizing this, the district attorney and the sheriff had purchased so much of the McKenzie 'shine that the owners started talking to them about becoming partners.

There was even a plan to take Parker and Devers to the location of the still to see the whole operation.

This was in May 1914; during this time, Parker and Devers also had a couple of detectives on the river acting as fishermen to watch for any suspicious activity. The detectives didn't spot the moonshiners, but one night, they heard people crossing the river. In the morning, they searched around and found the remains of the furnace, but the rest of the still was gone. The moonshiners must have caught wind of the fact that they were dealing with the authorities and decided to move the still before they were caught. Johnson S. Smith and C.A. Rudd, two revenue officers, expressed their frustration about how elusive they were by stating that "no Kentucky moonshiner ever was more keen in evading the officers of the law."

The next chance the authorities would get to try to capture the moonshiners was in June 1915. The detectives used the fisherman ruse again: two officers on the river with poles and a boat pretending to be fishermen. This time, they set up their headquarters twenty-six miles up the river from Springfield, between Deerhorn and Leaburg. For the first week, the officers went fishing for clues to catch the moonshiners, but the only thing they caught was fish. Not a bad gig; how many people get lucky enough to have their job not only encourage them to go fishing but also pay them to do so?

Eventually, their plan paid off, and the officers felt like they had found a location that might lead to the moonshiners. It was at a bend in the river, where the water was not too swift, a spot where even rowboats could be navigated without fear. The officers suspected this spot because they noticed that every time they approached this area, they would see another man on a boat following them.

The officers did not want the man in that boat to know what they were up to. So, one day, they went farther up the river from the bend and parked their boat. Then they trekked through the woods to get to the spot where they suspected the operation might be. Their hunch was correct, and they found parts of an abandoned still, with evidence that it had been in operation

A bend in the river. *Author's collection.*

recently. They also saw markings that made them believe that the still had been moved there not long ago. The following day, they decided to check the other side of the river to see if that was where the still used to be set up.

On the other side of the river, they found a large vat with a mixture of ground oats and corn that was fermenting in water. The only thing they did not find there was the kettle, but they did see a place that was set up for where the kettle would go. The moonshiners themselves continued to be elusive.

The main moonshiners in this operation were Mark Broom and James Williams. Williams was supposedly from Georgia, and it was said that Mark Broom, originally from Arkansas. had brought him over to Oregon to start their little illegal liquor business.

Mark lived with a family in Springfield. His father died a violent death. Mark was quoted in the *Morning Oregonian* as saying, "Ol' man war [was] shot up down in Arkansas." The newspapers stated that there were no records of whether or not he was killed in a feud but that Mark had said his father "war [was] an Arkansas Mountaineer." Mark was a plain man with a clean-shaven appearance. The newspapers noted that neither man had whiskers like the classic characters in tales of moonshiners.

James Williams had a prominent mole under his right eye. He lived in the mountains, and while he was able to keep himself clean-shaven, his hair was another story. What hair he had was unkempt and wild. His appearance was similar to the *Crook County Journal*'s description of the area where he lived: "rugged and wild."

Now that the authorities had part of the distillery, they believed they had enough to pursue arresting the moonshiners. They already knew who the moonshiners were from the previous year, when James Parker and J.M. Devers were buying the untaxed alcohol from them.

The hunt for the two didn't last too long, because Sheriff James Parker received a mysterious message that said Broom would leave Springfield for the McKenzie at a given time in the morning. Sheriff Parker jumped into an automobile at three fifteen in the morning to try to catch Mark Broom. The sheriff did spot him out on the road and attempted to get him to pull over, but Broom kept going. This car chase, which the *Sunday Oregonian* referred to as "sensational," lasted for over twenty miles.

The biggest fear for the sheriff was that Mark Broom would pull onto one of the roads leading into the mountains. Broom had been running a still in different parts of these woods that follow the McKenzie for nearly five years and knew his way around. If he got on one of those roads, Parker would have a hard time keeping up with him.

A road that follows the McKenzie River. *Author's collection.*

The chase must have been harrowing. The makes and models of the vehicles are unknown, but both men were driving cars that were made in 1915 or before. The chances that both had brand-new cars are low, and even if they did, the suspension, steering and braking technology at that time was rough at best. If they had Model Ts—the most popular car at the time— neither one would have had a fuel gauge, so running out of gas was always a possibility, especially going at high speeds. How much experience did they have with speeding? Did they know how much gas that would burn? Were they able to estimate how far they could go at high speeds?

The automobiles at that time were slow. Yes, the Model T could do forty miles per hour in the perfect scenario, but they were driving on rural roads in vehicles with limited suspension and tires that were only a few inches wide.

After nearly twenty miles of this, the sheriff was finally able to overtake Broom's automobile. This is where the story could have gotten violent, because Broom was heavily armed. Also, it turned out that James Williams was also in Broom's vehicle, so it was two against one. Luckily for the sheriff, Broom and Williams submitted to the arrest without resisting any further.

According to the *Sunday Oregonian*, the sheriff found a five-gallon keg of moonshine. Some newspapers had the number as high as fifteen gallons of moonshine plus two flasks. Parker was quoted as saying, "We can tell it is moonshine whiskey because there is none other like it." It was also said that the moonshiners called it "White Mule" whiskey because of its "kick."

After the bust, the sheriff told the papers about the pursuit of these two: "We knew they were doing it all the time. Harry Bown, Sheriff before my time, raided a still and got part of the outfit five years ago, but he lacked the necessary evidence." The sheriff went on to tell how he knew of seventy-five gallons of 'shine that had been made in their stills in the last month. Then the sheriff claimed that he already had two confessions and had the complete "goods" on them.

Once arrested, the two wouldn't spend too much time in Lane County. As federal prisoners, they were taken up to Portland by Deputy United States Marshal Tinnies De Boest. In Portland, they would be put in front of Assistant United States Attorney Robert R. Rankin before being arraigned by United States Commissioner Drake, who set their bail at $200 each. Rankin told the press that the moonshine that was seized was "Mighty Good Stuff….Tests have shown that it is 100 proof good" and it had that "real old moonshine flavor."

James Williams and Mark Broom were arrested in July, but their trial did not happen until December. Plenty of time to find a few witnesses.

During Assistant United States Attorney Rankin's opening statement, he told the court he would show that Mark Broom and James Williams had been operating a still making moonshine and selling it around Leaburg and Springfield. He also went on to say that Mark Broom had sent to Georgia for Williams to help set up and run their moonshine operation. Later in the trial, he would have local merchant W.B. Scott take the stand and testify that years before, he had loaned Broom seventy-five dollars, and he believed that Broom used it to bring James Williams to Oregon from Georgia.

William Martin, the council for Broom and Williams, said, "I don't believe that Mark Broom ever made a drop of whiskey in his life, nor even stirred the fire under the still that manufactured it."

James Parker, the Lane County sheriff who arrested the two men, was put on the stand. He was asked about catching the men, but defense attorney W.T. Vaughn objected that this was not related to the operation of the still and the manufacture and sale of liquor. The court sustained. Rankin then moved his questions to ones relative to the still and the selling of the liquor.

The prosecution's star witness was next to take the stand. His name was given as Teddy Doyle. Teddy was a nineteen-year-old who helped the moonshiners in their operation. In his testimony, he confessed to helping to haul, assemble and even operate the still. Here is his testimony describing the still:

An unknown man, circa 1925, sitting amid his distilling operation. The photo was reportedly taken in the woods near Vida, Oregon, another town along the McKenzie River. *Courtesy of the Lane County History Museum.*

Down from the hill a little stream of water ran in a trough and into a box filled with pipes. There was a big pot on a rock and mud bed with a place underneath to fire, a pipe led from the pot or boiler to the pipes in the box and besides the pot was a large bin for mixing the mash.

Teddy was asked what James Williams's occupation was, and he answered "moonshiner." Teddy seemed to have no problem singing like a canary. He told the court that last spring, they moved the still from the Jones place to a small canyon near Ward's Landing and that the two defendants helped put the plant together. He also said there was a third man, Sam Gott, whom he claimed had started the still with him. Teddy further admitted to stirring the mash, as well as hauling cornmeal and rye to the plant.

After Teddy was done spilling the beans, he was given a flask on the stand and told to look at it and smell it. Teddy looked at the flask, took a whiff of its contents and then, with a smile on his face, said, "That's like the whisky they made and it smells like it."

Sam Gott was up next on the stand. Sam corroborated what Teddy said and admitted his part in the operation. He told the court that he never got paid. Sam said that he "just helped them out because I kinder liked the stuff." He even admitted to drinking the product with Broom. Gott claimed that James Williams had told him that they had applied for a license.

John Doyle, Teddy's father, was a witness. He collaborated his son's story as well and admitted to hauling gallons of "the stuff" from Ward's Landing to Springfield, where it was stored.

Their trial ended on December 22, 1915. James Williams and Mark Broom were found guilty. Broom was sentenced to six months and a $500 fine. Williams received a nine-month sentence and a $500 fine. Judge Charles E. Wolverton said that he gave Williams and Broom a light sentence on the recommendation of the jury.

Williams and Broom were more than likely the last moonshiners to be busted while alcohol was still legal, since Oregon went dry less than two weeks later, on January 1, 1916, when the Anderson Act went into effect.

Mark Broom and Williams were asked if they had anything to say. Mark Broom stated

Judge Charles E. Wolverton. His family immigrated to the Oregon Territory in 1853. *From History of the Bench and Bar of Oregon (1910).*

that he was not guilty, but he would quit drinking. James Williams admitted his guilt but said he would never do it again.

They would do it again—this time, during Prohibition. In 1923, the *Oregon Statesman* ran an article with the headline "Large Moonshine Still Taken Near McKenzie." Deputy sheriffs raided the moonshine operation with a warrant for Williams and Broom. The two got away by running into the thick timber. John Broom, Mark's brother, was not so lucky. He was caught by authorities as he was running down a trail to get away. The article mentioned that the authorities had been trying to catch Mark Broom since the previous year, when he was accused of operating another still on the McKenzie near the Hendricks Bridge. For some people, moonshining is a way of life.

PART II

OREGON GOES DRY

Chapter 4

THE PENDLETON ESCAPE ARTIST, OR KING OF THE MOONSHINERS

O f all the moonshiners that operated in Oregon, Benjamin Franklin Jarrell is the most famous, but his fame does not stem from his moonshining; it's from his fiddle playing and singing in the short-lived but influential country group known as the Da Costa's Southwest Broadcasters. This group is considered important to the history of county music and was even featured in the Pioneers of Country Music trading cards that were drawn by legendary counterculture comic artist R. Crumb. Ben Jarrell has also been written about in many books and websites. But his moonshine career is rarely mentioned. If it is brought up at all, it's in the form of the simple narrative that Jarrell spent three years in Oregon, eighteen months of that in jail. Here, at last, is the full story of Benjamin Franklin Jarrell, fiddler, singer, husband, store owner, postmaster and, as he was known in Oregon, King of the Moonshiners.

Ben Jarrell was born in Round Peak, North Carolina. His father, Rufus Austin Jarrell, ran a licensed distillery. Jarrell, with pride, told a reporter, "My father ran a licensed distillery for 26 years and all the government officials who came to our place to gauge his liquor said he made the best brandy in the state." Jarrell also told the reporter that "I worked for him from the time I was a youngster till I was a man grown." During that time, his father instilled in him the idea that you should always turn out a product that you can be proud of. His brandy was known for its flavor, purity and strength. No adulterates were allowed, and the distillery was made of only the finest

An older Ben Jarrell holds his fiddle in this photo from his later music career. *Author's collection.*

materials—no cast iron or galvanized steel. Rufus knew it was important to use copper to make good liquor that wouldn't poison customers. When Ben got into moonshining, he did it by the same principles.

Ben made liquor in North Carolina up until his state's prohibition. Here he is in his own words, describing why he originally stopped making liquor in a prison interview with local journalist Fred Lockley from the *Oregon Daily Journal*: "I kept up moonshining till North Carolina voted for prohibition, and then I quit, because I believe in the rule of the majority, and I wouldn't go against the express will of the fellow citizens of my state."

Later in the interview, Lockley asked Jarrell how he began moonshining and why he came to Oregon:

> *How did I happen to come out to Oregon and get caught making moonshine? I was running a store back home and was too easy, giving credit to the folks I had been raised with. I couldn't bear to turn them down when they said "Just charge it." I finally got in debt over six thousand dollars. I can't abide not being able to settle my obligations, so I came out here to make some big money quick to get my debts cleaned up. I figured if the people out here were bound to get whiskey I would furnish it to them a good turn by making a high grade of genuine moonshine instead of the hair oil, varnish and pain killers they are using but the officers didn't agree with me; so here I am.*

In North Carolina, good liquor was going for $1.00 to $1.50 per gallon. In Oregon, now that Prohibition was in effect, garbage bathtub liquor was going for $10 to $12 per quart. If Jarrell wanted to raise enough money to get out of debt, Oregon was the place to do it.

Part of the reason booze was worth so much in Oregon is that the state was early to the Prohibition party. Oregon was dry as of 1914. At that time, it was still legal to go to another state, bring liquor back and drink it in your own home. In 1916, this loophole was closed, and Oregon became quite parched.

Around this time, Ben Jarrell started coming to Oregon to help the state's thirsty souls, and he made good money doing it. On his first trip to Oregon, after his expenses, he made $1,100 making liquor after just four days of work. In the latter part of 1917, he made his second trip to the state. This time, he brought out two sixty-five-gallon copper stills. With them, he was able to make forty-five gallons a day. In less than two weeks, he made and sold what he had and headed back to North Carolina, this time with $2,300.

A popular saying is that the third time's the charm, but it wasn't for Jarrell. On his third trip to Oregon, he was hoping to make $5,000 and then call it quits as a moonshiner—enough money to pay off his debts and get slightly ahead. In his words, he wanted to have "ready money." But that trip was the first time Jarrell was caught in Oregon.

With him, on this trip, he brought his twenty-seven-year-old neighbor Sam Holden to help him with the operation. He also hired a local named Bill Clark, the twenty-four-year-old son of a rancher, to do the rougher work.

Now, sometimes your smarts can get you in trouble, or maybe breaking the law and trying to get away with it is just a recipe for failure. Jarrell knew that sometimes people would get caught when they were seen buying supplies that could be used for making illegal liquor. To try to get around this, he hired another local, name unknown, to buy the supplies. Only this runner ended up leading the authorities to them. Jarrell was right that liquor-making supplies were being monitored, because the law first got wind of his operation from a Walla Walla merchant who alerted the authorities that someone had bought a large quantity of cornmeal. Then one day, Jarrell's runner was bringing the supplies up to the operation in exchange for his own five gallons of liquor. With him was a man who was supposedly just another thirsty soul but turned out to be an undercover government official. It wasn't long after that incident that Sheriff Tilman "Til" Taylor and a posse of thirteen men showed up at the operation late one night.

Sheriff Til was a seasoned lawman. He was sixteen years into his eighteen-year career when he first went after Jarrell. It was said that during his career, he arrested 2,600 men. Til was not a hated lawman; he was generally liked even by the people he captured. Bob Stangier from the Umatilla County historical society, whose father knew Til, said that "he could arrest his best friend and they'd still be friends at the end of the occasion." Stangier also said that "[Til] could arrest a total stranger and they'd end up friends." This does seem to be true, because you will see during this story that Jarrell might have been busted by Til, but he respected him nonetheless.

The three men operating the still had a gun each, but Sheriff Til was coming for them with a large posse of deputized men—a large enough group that they needed three vehicles. Some of the men included Captain Williams and Deputy Game Warden Averill.

The men drove as close as they could get to the still, about two miles out. Then they walked the rest of the way up the steep grade. It was said that there were no trails or paths to be found to aid them. The still had been operating for some time, and Til had made the trip out to the still a number

Til Taylor on a horse in Pendleton. *Courtesy of the Umatilla County Historical Society.*

of times in the week leading up to this raid, so they had a good idea where they were heading, at least. The still was located on top of a hill and hidden by sagebrush. The posse saw no signs of the distillery until they were within thirty feet of it. Then they could see the fire burning underneath the furnace in the still operation. The process was at the point that the steam was curling through the "worm" and the liquor was flowing into the collection bucket.

The moonshiners had no idea the raid was coming. They thought they were perfectly safe. One of them, Sam Holden or Bill Clark, later said, "I thought I was as safe as I would have been in my own home." Ben Jarrell, the leader of the operation, was spotted when the posse got close enough to peek through the sagebrush. Jarrell was lying down, asleep, with his rifle at his side. The other two men were sitting by the fire with rifles on their laps.

The posse hit the little camp all at once. They were able to get Jarrell's gun and subdue him right away. Sam Holden thought about shooting his way out, and he even reached for his gun three times, but seeing that he was surrounded, he opted to leave it where it lay. Bill Clark gave the officers no resistance in his arrest.

What happened next is best described in Ben Jarrell's own words:

> *I was kind of provoked because he* [Sheriff Til] *didn't take my word, so I decided to quit the bunch. They made a little campfire near the autos and as we sat around the fire we all took a few drinks from the keg they had brought along as evidence. I think all drank but Til. He wasn't thirsty, he said. As they were all talking about what good luck they had in nabbing us I made a sudden dive like a cottontail into a bunch of small pines. There was a hummock about forty to fifty feet from the fire. I dropped at full length behind that.*

Jarrell figured they would assume he ran off like a "scared coyote," and he was right; they thought he ran far. So they ran far looking for him. Now, most people, after pulling off this trick, would have jumped up as soon as the posse was out of sight and make their escape. Most people making that decision would be spotted and caught. Jarrell took the chance that if they didn't find him on their way past, they probably wouldn't find him on the way back. It was a risk on his part but a risk that worked out in his favor. He lay there as the posse walked back to the campsite—a campsite he was close enough to that he could hear them talking about him.

Jarrell said that when the posse came back, they sat around the fire talking about how fast he must have run. He said that Sheriff Til even said, "No use

Til Taylor proudly holding a small barrel of captured moonshine. *Courtesy of the Umatilla County Historical Society.*

cussing about him. It was our own fault. I don't blame him any. I would have done the same thing."

Once the posse left, Jarrell started his long escape to Idaho. First, he went to Heppner and stayed in a hotel for a week, waiting for things to calm down. Before Jarrell left Heppner, he switched to different clothes and bought new shoes and a different-looking hat. Then he went to the train depot to make his escape. The train was searched, but Jarrell wasn't discovered. While he was on the train, he found out that every ferry and road was supposedly guarded. With this information, Jarrell made his plan. First, he hired an unlicensed taxi—or, as it was called at that time, a jitney—to take him out to see what kind of land there was around Arlington. Jarrell most likely didn't care to see Arlington but just wanted time to build some trust with the jitney operator before he asked him to do something that would seem questionable.

Once Jarrell felt comfortable with the jitney operator, he offered him a generous tip to take him on board the ferry in his vehicle, in order to get Jarrell to the other side with fewer eyes on him. The jitney operator agreed, and the plan worked. Jarrell got himself out of Oregon. From there, he took a train to Spokane and then made his way to Sanders, Idaho, where an old neighbor of his lived.

This is the point in the story where you must question the intelligence that everyone said Jarrell had, because Sheriff Til found him, and even though Til had no authority in Idaho, Jarrell ended up letting Til take him back to Oregon. Here is how it went down. Til showed up at the place Jarrell was staying, along with the local authority, Sheriff Nowlin. Luckily for Jarrell, he was out hunting at the time, and Til and Nowlin didn't bother hanging around, but Til did leave a message for Jarrell, telling Jarrell to call him. Jarrell called; Til wasn't there. Jarrell left him a message for Til to call him back. Five minutes later, Til called Jarrell back and told him that it would be better for him to get arrested out here than back at home in North Carolina where everyone knew him. Til said that it would save a lot of expense if Jarrell would surrender. Jarrell thought about this and agreed, telling Til that he would go with him if Til showed up by himself, without the local authorities. Til agreed, and Jarrell said that he knew Til he wouldn't lie to him because Til was a Mason, like himself.

As Jarrell was quoted as saying, Til played it square with Jarrell, so Jarrell played square with him and traveled back to Oregon without issue. Jarrell even offered to pay for his own train ticket back. Til told Jarrell that he might as well save his money and paid for both of their tickets.

Above: George Washington was a Mason. *Courtesy of Sandy Historical Society.*

Opposite: A statue of Til Taylor was erected in 1929. *Author's collection.*

While Jarrell was on the run, his two cohorts were taken to Portland, where they were convicted and sentenced. Sam Holden and Bill Clark each received thirty days in jail and had to pay a $500 fine. Jarrell ended up getting six months in jail. Once he got out, he didn't want to go back to North Carolina empty-handed, so he started up another still.

NO. 51. TIL TAYLOR STATUE, PENDLETON, OREGON.

This time, Jarrell's operation was in Astoria, Oregon. He was again busted, and while he was incarcerated, he heard that Til Taylor was killed in the line of duty, during a jailbreak. Jarrell was saddened by the news and sent a contribution of five dollars to the Til Taylor memorial fund. With his contribution, he included a letter: "Included you will find $5—the best I can do. I cannot express how sorry I was to hear of his tragic end. It is a shame that a brave, good man like Til Taylor should have been shot from behind by a dirty cur."

This time in prison seems to have been the last for Jarrell. When he got out, he moved back to North Carolina but didn't forget about his time in Oregon. In 1921, he wrote a letter to Fred Lockley, who had interviewed him while he was in prison. Here is that letter from Ben Jarrell, the King of the Moonshiners, reflecting on his time in Oregon:

My Dear Mr. Lockley: I would like to be in old Portland today, but not where you met me. I guess you are guessing where you met me. It was in the jail, and if you are guessing my name, it is Ben Jarrell, the man you wrote up in The Journal. *I was known in your county as the King of the Moonshiners. Here I am known as Mr. B.F. Jarrell. Mr. Lockley, somehow I got to thinking of you today, so I decided to write you so you would not think I was always engaged in the moonshining industry. I wish you would convey my best regard to the sheriff and to George Hurlburt, and will you tell Charles Reames I feel very thankful to him for what he did for me, and I want you to know how thankful I felt to you for the big bunch of books you brought me while I was in jail. I have a nice business here and I believe I will do well. Sometime write me a line or so, for I liked Oregon pretty well if they hadn't pestered me so much. If you don't get time to write, send me a late copy of* The Journal *and I will read it all through and get a line on how things are going out there. Very truly yours, B.F. Jarrell.*

CHAPTER 5

A CLACKAMAS LEGEND AND QUEEN OF THE MOONSHINERS

Of all the moonshiners written about in this book, Nettie Connett has received more ink than any of them. She was a legend in Clackamas County and was written about in many of the local papers and some out-of-state papers, as well. These papers didn't just write about her getting in trouble for manufacturing moonshine liquor. She was a real character, and everyone knew about her exploits. This remains true to this day; though she passed nearly sixty years ago, people still know her name. She was such a legend that, posthumously, the town of Sandy, Oregon, named a road after her. Though she lived in Aims, Oregon, most of her business and social life revolved around the town of Sandy.

With all these articles written about Nettie, many words have been used to describe her. Here is a portion of them: dairymaid, mother, midwife, waitress, restaurateur, hotelier, sharpshooter, trapper, timber dealer, logger, cattle raiser, horse breeder, fun seeker, tobacco user, the user of profanity, hellraiser and, of course, moonshiner.

Nettie was born in 1880 in Independence, Oregon, to William and Harriet "Hattie" Connett. Nettie was the fourth child out of ten to be born to this couple. This was the second marriage for the Iowa-born William. His first marriage produced one boy and one girl. Harriett was eighteen years old when they married. She was born in 1855 in what was then called the Oregon Territory. Her original last name was Cook. The two stayed married for the rest of William's life; he died in 1905, and Harriet passed in 1939.

A proud Nettie Connett. *Courtesy of Sandy Historical Society.*

She never remarried; her simple stone grave marker still bears the last name of her husband, who died so many years before her.

Nettie's true first name is Annette, but she always went by Nettie. Nettie attended school in Independence and Sweet Home, Oregon. In 1893, when she was about thirteen years of age, she made the list of children in her school who hadn't been tardy or had any absences. Nettie had a short school career, though. From an early age, she had a smoking habit, and this would eventually lead to the end of her school days. When she found out that a teacher had heard about her smoking, she decided to stop going. She was quoted as saying she was afraid they would "lick me when I came back to school." So, in her words, "I fooled them, he had never seen me since, 'cause I never went to school another day."

By the age of eighteen, Nettie was married to William Dempsey, a man twenty years her senior. She had one child with him; they named the boy William. Nettie and William started their life together in Waterloo, Oregon. The relationship didn't last long. Later in life, Nettie would be quoted as saying, "Lost my husband in Waterloo, he didn't die. I just told him to 'get lost' because he didn't treat me right."

After this, Nettie moved to Portland to try her luck at city life. Her first job was as a waitress; eventually, she would own her own restaurant. Later, she took over the restaurant in the Ohio Hotel; she ran the restaurant so well that she convinced the owner she could run the hotel as well, and they became partners.

City life wouldn't last long for Nettie. In November 1909, a marriage announcement was published in the *Morning Oregonian*. It said that Leroy E. Seeley and Miss Nettie L. Connett, both of this city, were married at one thirty yesterday afternoon, at the home of the bride's mother, Hattie L. Connett, 172 Grand Avenue North. The little marriage announcement also stated that the two would reside in Tokeland, Washington, where the groom would be associated in business with his father, F.E. Seeley, who was a successful logging operator in western Washington.

This marriage must not have lasted long, as Nettie never mentioned it in any of the interviews she gave in her life. This short marriage might be how she learned about the logging industry, because a year later, Nettie, as she put it, "Took to the Woods."

Nettie sold her interest in the Ohio hotel and bought a tract of timber in Clackamas County, near Bull Run and Aims, Oregon. Nettie became a logger and timber dealer, sometimes selling the lumber and sometimes selling the land itself. Nettie claimed to have sold some two thousand acres in half a century. Rural life suited Nettie, and this is when her life got interesting and she got to be exactly who she wanted to be.

Unless she was going to a wedding or a funeral, Nettie felt most comfortable in the clothing associated with the loggers she worked among. Her standard outfit was jeans, boots and a beat-up red felt cap. Their attire was not the only thing that Nettie learned from the loggers. It was said by some that Nettie was a crude woman who chewed tobacco and used much profanity or, as some people called it, "logger talk."

One profanity-filled incident was the time Nettie ran into Dr. Hughes from Gresham, who was on a call. When he saw Nettie approaching from the rear of his horse and buggy, he motioned for her to pass on by. Nettie didn't appreciate his politeness, and she let him have it with a string of

Nettie Connett loved to hunt. *Courtesy of Sandy Historical Society.*

obscenities, letting him know that she didn't need special treatment just because she was a woman. Dr. Hughes was a beloved doctor in the area and was well-liked enough to become mayor of Gresham and hold the position for sixteen years.

A similar incident happened to a man named Jack Warner, who came across Nettie along a trail. Warner, trying to be polite, stepped to the side for her to pass, and when he did, he received the typical Nettie response of many harsh words and the statement that she was no lady and "could hold her own with any man in any contest."

But there was another side to Nettie, because there are just as many stories of her bringing food to neighbors in need or loaning money to people to whom most would not. She was also one who was always willing to make contributions to community projects.

The woods and the land provided much for Nettie. She made her money from logging and selling land, and she even had some cattle and pigs. Nettie also became an avid hunter and trapper. She had hunting dogs and was known to hunt and trap various animals, including cougars, bobcats, deer and even bears.

Another way Nettie made money, of course, was making moonshine. Her first bust was on November 6, 1919, two months prior to the Volstead Act going into effect. But of course, alcohol was already illegal in Oregon. Rumor had it that most of Nettie's product was sold out of a garage in the neighboring town north of Aims, called Springdale.

When Clackamas County sheriff William Wilson and his deputies, A.G Metades, Henry Hughes and one revenue agent, arrived on

A rare photo of Nettie Connett in fancy clothes. A story often told about Nettie is that a friend once saw her in a dress at a wedding, and when the person asked Nettie where her jeans were, she pulled her dress up to reveal she had them on underneath. *Courtesy of Sandy Historical Society.*

Sheriff William Wilson. *Courtesy of the Clackamas County Sheriff's Office.*

Nettie's property, they were surprised by how accommodating she was. She was dressed in overalls and had a jovial attitude, and she welcomed them all. The *Oregon City Enterprise*, quoted her as saying, "Walk right in and take a look."

At first, the house seemed like any old farmhouse, until they found the still located in the basement. This still had a novel feature: a thirty-foot pipe that led from the attic to the basement. It was a feeder for the mash that was in the attic. The room that the mash was in had its floor tinned over. Later, Nettie would tell different stories about the setup. One was that the setup was already there when she moved in. She claimed that she thought the tinned-floor room was for drying fruit. The other explanation she gave was that one of her workers had set the still up, and she fired him when she found out about it.

According to the *Oregon City Enterprise* article, Nettie's spirits were high during the search and the arrest. She treated the incident as a joke, going so far as to laugh at how long she had gotten away with moonshining without getting caught.

One of the officers let it slip that they were going to bust a still in Sandy after hers. Nettie wanted to go along; she told the officer, "Is that so? Take me along. I bet you he don't make as good a showing as I did."

A man named Everett Lowther, who was on her property, was also arrested at the time. Lowther and Nettie were brought along for the ride to their next bust. The still was a small operation, as Nettie had described it. Clarence Cassidy was the alleged moonshiner. His still was in his basement, as well. He, too, was arrested and brought in with the other two. It was said that Nettie "kidded" him that his outfit was nothing compared to hers. Her still was a bigger operation; they caught her with one hundred gallons of mash. Cassidy's was a smaller operation, and they only found fifty gallons of mash on his property.

After this first bust, Nettie was given a trial before Justice of the Peace Levy Stipp at the justice court. She was found guilty and fined one hundred dollars. Everett Lowther pleaded not guilty. Both would still have to face federal court. During the preliminary hearing before United States Commissioner Frederick H. Drake, Lowther would be discharged for lack of evidence.

During Nettie's trial, it was said that she had a jaunty attitude. According to reports, she was unabashed by the situation. She denied all charges and told the court that two hired hands set up the still operation and she discharged both when she found out.

Unluckily for her, the prosecution was able to find a witness who claimed that Nettie did run the operation. One of the stories he told became the headline for an article about her trial: "Hogs' Tipsy Revel Reveals Big Still." This story was also picked up in a Montana newspaper with the headline: "Pigs Get Soused on Mash; Squeal and Walk Zig Zag." A.W. Brewer was the witness's name, and he claimed that one of his jobs on her property was "slipping the hawgs." Brewer's story was that he found various barrels of discarded mash set aside for hog feed. He noticed after the feeding that when the hogs were let out to the pasture, they had an "uncertain, shuffling gait." Further damning testimony from Brewer was that he claimed Nettie had given him little bottles of moonshine on two occasions and that she had shown him the still. He also claimed that she had him stir the mash on occasion. His testimony also incriminated Everett Lowther, as he claimed that Everett was there when Nettie showed him the still.

The trial lasted two days, and Nettie was found guilty on three counts: distilling liquor, paying no revenue tax and possession of a still ready for operation. Nettie was given thirty days to appeal before sentencing. She was released on $1,500 bail. Eventually, she would be sentenced to six months and a $500 fine. With appeals and additional bonds, she was able to keep herself out of jail for quite a while.

Within a week of Nettie's trial ending, she was arrested. She was caught, again with Everett Lowther, with liquor in an automobile. Constable Squires was the arresting officer.

Once free, Nettie got straight back to work producing more liquor. This time, she did not make the amateur mistake of building a still inside her own home. Her new operation was estimated to have cost around $1,500 to construct, and this time, it was all underground.

This still was raided as well. It was in September 1920; the Volstead Act had been in effect since January 17 of that year. Sheriff Wilson was again the lead officer on the search of Nettie's property and was the one to find the opening of her homemade distillery. The still was on the edge of her property, about seventy-five yards from the property of her neighbor George Wilkinson. Near the creek was a big slope, and hidden behind some ferns, Wilson discovered a door. Behind that door was a fifteen-foot-long tunnel that led to a strong locked door. Wilson cautiously entered the tunnel and made his way to the locked door. The officers had to break down the door to gain entry. Once opened, it revealed a rather large, planked, sixteen-by-ten-foot underground cave with a ninety-gallon copper still. They found a pipe hidden in hollow logs that ran water from a creek that was five hundred feet away. They also discovered one hundred feet of insulated wire that they believed was going to be used to build an alert system. When Nettie was first busted, the newspapers were impressed by her operation. That first operation was nowhere near as sophisticated as this one. This time, the officers also didn't just find a still and a little bit of mash; this time, they found five hundred gallons of mash and ten gallons of finished liquor. After this bust, the *Morning Oregonian* gave Nettie the sensational name Queen of the Moonshiners. No one was home during the search, so no arrests were made at that point.

The still was dismantled and hauled off the property. Sheriff Wilson had half of the distillery attached to the front of his police vehicle. While he was driving away, he passed another vehicle on the road. Everett Lowther was the driver, with Nettie Connett and her neighbor George Wilkinson as passengers. By the time the sheriff was able to turn his car around and chase after them, they had gotten a substantial lead. Once they were far enough ahead, they pulled to the side of the road, where Nettie and George ran into the woods. The sheriff waited for them to come back out, but they never did. Lowther, who stayed in the car, claimed that Nettie and George were never in the car.

There is another legend, never reported to the papers but passed down through time from person to person. It concerns the time Nettie was stopped while making a moonshine run to Oregon City. According to legend, Nettie had just left her property with a load of moonshine, heading to Oregon City to unload it to a buyer out there. On her way, she was stopped by two officers, who asked her if she knew Nettie Connett. Being that they were talking about her, this piqued her curiosity. So, she asked them why they were looking for Nettie. They told her that it was suspected that she was involved in the illegal manufacture of liquor. Then, according to the legend, Nettie gave the officers instructions on how to get to her place. Once they were on their way, she continued her trip to Oregon City and sold off the moonshine.

Nettie remained free another month before she was arrested on a bench warrant that was issued after a secret indictment by the grand jury. The charge was violating the Federal Prohibition Act.

Nettie continued to keep herself out of any real time in jail by paying her appeal bonds. The first was $1,500, the second was $500 and the third was $1,250. Eventually, she ran out of appeals, and Nettie had to serve her six months in jail, which she began in May 1921.

Nettie Connett sitting on top of a large stack of lumber. *Courtesy of Sandy Historical Society.*

After Nettie got out, she must have given up on the moonshine game or found out how to not get caught, because there are no more references in the newspapers to Nettie making booze after this. There are plenty of other Nettie stories, though. Nettie was just getting into her forties at this point.

Nettie was a legendary hunter, and it was claimed that whatever season it was, Nettie would always be the first back in town with an animal strapped to her green Studebaker pickup truck. Usually, she would go by a few different places with her trophy. One would be the school. The teachers didn't mind the kids coming out and seeing whatever she happened to have shot, be it a cougar, bobcat, deer or, if the kids were lucky, a bear. The only thing the teachers requested of Nettie was not to use any of her "logger talk" around the children.

Nettie would also stop by Irene's bar. Irene's, also known as Good Night, Irene's, was the bar that Nettie called her office. It was where she went to socialize and where she would meet people to sell off land or timber. It is also where, on her birthday, well into her seventies, she would do a handstand on the barstool just to show that she still could.

The Sandy Outlook was also a usual stopping point for Nettie with her recent capture. There were many articles over the years about Nettie and

Nettie Connett sitting at a bar. *Courtesy of Sandy Historical Society.*

the animals she hunted. In 1957, when she was seventy-seven years old, she got herself a four-point blacktail weighing 185 pounds. It was said in the article that this was her sixtieth year of hunting. That story ran in papers all over the country, including California, New Mexico, Texas, Minnesota, Nebraska, Kansas, Illinois, Kentucky and even Alabama. The following year, some of those papers also ran a photo of Nettie doing her annual birthday barstool handstand.

Another thing Nettie was known for was her poor driving skills, and they would lead to her end. She drove an old Studebaker pickup, and it was said that kids would jump into the ditches whenever they saw her driving down the road. According to others, she drove in the middle of the road, making people swerve to miss hitting her. At age eighty-four, Nettie backed out of Irene's into the road without looking. Her vehicle was struck by a logging truck. She spent the next five months in a care facility before passing on. Though she has passed, the legend of Nettie continues. There are many tales about her that are still told, and according to her, when asked to verify the wild claims, she would always respond, "They are all true! Whatever they say about me is so!"

CHAPTER 6

FLEGEL'S SEARCH FOR THE AUSTRIAN MOONSHINE RING

Assistant Attorney Austin Flegel Jr. had the theory that there was an Austrian moonshine ring operating in Oregon. In an article titled "Moonshine Inquiry Promises Sensation," Flegel told the *Morning Oregonian* that 75 percent of all moonshining cases that had come across his desk in the last few months had been Austrians. He claimed that in almost every case, bail had been furnished by a local Austrian, an individual Austin Flegel referred to as a "fixer." If there was a ring of Austrian moonshiners, only a few of them seemed to get caught in cases high-profile enough to make their way into the local papers.

The article that Flegel was interviewed for was about a big Austrian moonshine bust in April 1920 in the small sawmill town of Boring. The town of Boring was named after William Boring, who donated land for the first school in the area. More stories about the town of Boring can be read in *Eccentric Tales of Boring, Oregon*, from the same author and publisher. The bust was considered a big one. One article claimed that it was the largest still ever found in Clackamas County, possibly the biggest in the state.

The two supposed Austrians involved claimed to be cousins. They also claimed that they were both named Boze Yuginivic. The cousins Yuginivic rented a five-acre piece of property in Boring, where they set up an elaborate still with large vats and an underground piping system. One part of the still that impressed the arresting officers was an oil burner that could heat up two stills at the same time. The oil burner was said to be different from any yet found in Clackamas County, and they believed it was probably shipped from the East Coast.

Portland Archives, A2004-001.13.

MEMBERS OF THE CITY COUNCIL, PORTLAND, ORE.

No. 1—A. F. FLEGEL	No. 5—C. E. RUMELIN	No. 8—D. T. SHERRETT
No. 2—B. D. SIGLER	No. 6—L. ZIMMERMAN	No. 9—H. R. ALBEE
No. 3—MAT FOELLER	President of the Council	No. 10—F. T. MERRILL
No. 4—SANDFORD WHITING	No. 7—J. P. SHARKEY	No. 11—A. K. BENTLEY

Austin Flegel Jr. (*top left*). *Courtesy of City of Portland (OR) Archives, A2004-001.13.*

Sandy Historical Society
Photo - 1847

BORING

Original Boring Schoolhouse built in 1883 when William H. Boring donated land for the school

The town of Boring, Oregon, was named after William H. Boring, who donated the land for the first schoolhouse. *Courtesy of Sandy Historical Society.*

What made this such a big bust was the quantity of materials found and the quality of the setup. The raiding officers found 70 gallons of finished moonshine and 1,700 gallons of corn mash. It appeared that they had been at it for a while, though they claimed they had not been at the place long. The elaborate setup, plus the thirty-six empty sugar sacks and eleven empty kerosene cases, pointed otherwise.

The two-man operation was busted by Prohibition Agents Flanders and Kerfoot. With them were two local authorities, Sheriff Wilson and Deputy Sheriff Hughes. Sheriff Wilson had caught a few supposed Austrians the previous year. The first bust involved two men with twelve quarts of moonshine. The second man caught had seventy-five pints of moonshine. A month after that bust, Wilson and Hughes busted another farm run by three more supposed Austrians; those three had fifteen gallons hidden around their property in pint containers. None of these cases were connected to either of the Boze Yuginivics.

It's especially hard to make such connections when suspects are not using their real names. Once they were done with the courts and their fines in Boring, the Yuginivics moved their operation to Newberg, Oregon.

With the new location came new names: Boze Yuginivic number one, the manager of the operation, began using the name Bob Uger, and his supposed cousin, Boze Yuginivic number two, started using the name Mike Basich.

During their time operating the still in Newberg, another couple of men with the last name Basich were busted moving moonshine: James and John Basich. They claimed that they were not related. These Basichs were caught in possession of twenty-four pints of moonshine whiskey in a suitcase at the Oak Hotel in Portland. Later, Austin Flegel would tell the press that he believed he had found the Austrian moonshine ringleader, and his name was John Basich.

The Newberg still was another big operation that was estimated to be able to produce one hundred gallons a day. The moonshiners rented a bit of property and erected their own building for the operation. Their cover story with the landowners was that they were raising chickens and ducks for meat. In the front of the building was a living space for the two men. In the rear, they had a large coal oil–heated still with pressure tanks, giant vats for mash and a pump to bring water from a nearby stream. They had plenty of cornmeal as well as hops.

This operation didn't last long. They started construction in May, just after the Boring bust, and by August, they were raided once again. The raiding officers were Federal Prohibition Agent Edward Wolfe, Federal Inspector C.R. Stipe and Deputy Collector Asa Smith. Edward Wolfe had an interesting reputation. When he busted a still on the property of Stillman Andrews, he was allegedly drunk. At least, that is what Andrews told the jury during the trial, and they might just have believed him, because they found him not guilty.

Wolfe, Stipe and Smith headed out from Portland to Newberg on a tip that there was a moonshine operation on the Hall farm property. They started on the south side of his farm and moved north, which is where the still was located, but before they could reach it, they were spotted. There was a little shack on a hill that the moonshiners used as a lookout, and as soon as they saw the officers, they took off into the thick timber and were gone.

One member of the raiding party stayed behind and watched the property as the two other men went to get Sheriff Henderson. The sheriff came at once in his vehicle; with him were his son and three others: County Clerk C.B. Wilson, Marshal Ferguson and Oliver Evans, a photographer and writer for the *Newberg Graphic*. Lawrence Hall, seeing the commotion, made his way over to that side of his property with his son in tow.

Before the still was dismantled, Oliver Evans was allowed to take a photograph of it, though it was night and the still was lit only by a flashlight. The taking of the photograph was written about in the *Newberg Graphic*, but the paper never ran the photo.

The officers removed the copper still and took a few samples for evidence. With that done, they set the building on fire. With the coal oil and whiskey inside the building, it went up in smoke in no time. Drawn by the fire and all the excitement, many townspeople from Newberg came out. Some of them claimed that Asa Smith and Edward Wolfe were drunk off the captured moonshine. Wolfe claimed that he had only taken a drink from two of the containers to verify that it was in fact moonshine.

Lawrence Hall, the landowner, was taken to Portland for questioning. Bob Uger and Mike Basich were arrested later at 878 Union Avenue in North Portland, the residence of John Basich. Bob Uger and Mike Basich, just like they did during the Boring incident, told the officers that they were merely employees of the operation and refused to name any higher-ups. This would change with one of them when the case went to trial.

A couple of months later, Austin Flegel was able to build a big enough case to arrest John Basich on the charge of running the Newberg distillery. Flegel told the press that "the real man in the Newberg still case has been found." John Basich was said to be surprised; he believed that the state had no evidence against him. Flegel stated that he had gathered evidence from bootleggers and others. It was also revealed that John Basich had paid Bob Uger's and Mike Basich's fines.

The trial began in January 1921. The prosecution was being handled by Austin Flegel who said in his opening statement:

> *The government would show that Basich leased the property for no other purpose than the manufacture of liquor, built thereon his distillery, installed the still and delivered huge quantities of ingredients and employed two foreign workmen, Bob Uger and Mike Basich, at monthly salaries of $250 to operate the still. Both employees already have pleaded guilty to the charge of operating [and] have paid fines of $250 each. It is not the government's claim that John Basich did the work, he hired this done, but reaped the profits.*

The defense was handled by Barnett "Barney" Goldstein. Goldstein was a respected attorney. He was born in Russia, but he grew up in New York, and that is where he got his education. He attended the New York

Law School. Goldstein was admitted to the bar in New York in 1912 and then moved to Oregon to practice law in Portland. From 1916 to 1920, he was a U.S. attorney, before going into private law for financial reasons. Goldstein was a man well known in the city. He was a member of many clubs, including the Breakfast Club, Woodmen of the World and the Elks; he was an Eagle, a Scottish Rite Mason and a Shriner and, a couple of years after this trial, he became a member of the KGW Hoot Owls. The Hoot Owls was a popular local radio comedy program about a mythical fraternal lodge called the Hoot Owls, Goldstein was well known for playing the Grand Schmoos.

Barnett "Barney" Goldstein. *Courtesy of City of Portland (OR) Archives, A2000-026.266.*

C.R. Stipe, a federal Prohibition inspector who was at the Newberg bust, was put on the stand that day. His job was to identify the copper still as being from the Newberg operation. He was also there to testify about the specifics of the distillery. He described the operation in detail to the court, including the 800 gallons of mash and 250 gallons of moonshine whiskey found on the property.

The first day of the trial was a short day, because Goldstein asked for an adjournment, pleading that he was having throat trouble. Though the trial would end early that day, there still was some excitement. But it didn't happen in the courtroom. It happened in the hallway.

The big excitement that day was between Mike Mikolish and Mike Basich. Mikolish was a state witness in the case against John Basich. Mike Basich launched himself at Mikolish when he saw him and was quoted to have said, "I got a good notion to throw you from this here window" and "I tell you now. Mikolish, for your own good, if you testify against John this state will be too hot to hold you." Mike Basich was arrested on the charge of attempting to intimidate a witness. Austin Flegel was quick to comfort Mike Mikolish after the incident to make sure his witness stayed a witness.

When the trial resumed, one of the other witnesses to be called was ten-year-old Doris Miller. In her testimony, she told the courtroom how she was not allowed in the building where the distillery had been found. Doris had been told that the building was going to be used for housing and processing chickens and ducks. She thought this was odd, since she never saw any fowl around the building.

Doris Miller told the court how she had seen the men bring "funny looking stuff" to feed the pigs. She identified the "stuff" as cracked corn. The most damning part of her testimony was her statement that she saw John Basich on the property. He was there during the erection of the stillhouse, a fact that was also confirmed by Lawrence and Elmer Hall's testimony. They added that there were frequent visits to the farm by John, sometimes in an automobile and sometimes in a truck. Most of the visits were at night and many times, with the truck, he brought cracked corn.

Goldstein questioned Lawrence Hall about his testimony. He inferred that Austin Flegel had threatened Lawrence and Elmer. Lawrence Hall denied this and said that Flegel had simply "cautioned" him to tell the truth or he would be held liable for charges of perjury.

If Mike Basich was mad about Mike Mikolish testifying against John, he must have been furious when he found out his partner Bob Uger was going to be the last witness of the trial for the prosecution. Turning one of the moonshiners against the others was Austin Flegel's ace in the hole in winning this case.

The main road in Boring, Oregon, now part of Highway 212. *Courtesy of Sandy Historical Society.*

Uger confessed on the stand that Mike Basich and himself had built the building on the Hall property under John Basich's direction. Uger went on to explain that John supplied all the necessary provisions for the operation and the legal support. He confessed that they had made four to five hundred gallons of moonshine before they were busted. On the stand, Uger also brought up the operation in Boring, Oregon, and how when they got caught, John paid the fines as well as their attorney fees.

Goldstein cross-examined Uger and asked him why he hadn't told Judge Bean about John Basich during the Boring trial. Goldstein was Uger's attorney during that trial, and Goldstein had told the court then that he was unable to get any hint of who owned the still. So, Goldstein as well as the court was startled and confused when Uger replied, "You told him." Uger seemed to be trying to shift the blame from himself to his own lawyer by contradicting his statement and claiming that not only did Goldstein know who the leader was, but he had also told Judge Bean.

Austin Flegel may not have proven there was a large Austrian moonshine ring, but he did succeed in busting John Basich and connecting him to both the Newberg and Boring operations. John was found guilty by the jury on two counts: maintaining a nuisance and the manufacture of liquor. John was sentenced to one year's imprisonment and a $500 fine. Bob Uger and Mike Basich were fined $250 each for their part in the Newberg still.

PART III

SPEAKEASIES, SAKE AND SODA JERKS IN PORTLAND, OREGON

CHAPTER 7

SAKE MOONSHINE
IN OLD TOWN

O ne of the earliest illegal alcohol busts in the Portland area was downtown in what is known as the North End. This still was operating in what the *Morning Oregonian* called a tenement. It was near Third and Flanders. The still was not a typical corn or rye moonshine whiskey operation. This was a sake operation, and it was owned by K. Sumata.

Sumata's still was busted in March 1917. The still was found by accident when two patrolmen, William Miller and John Wellbrook, were going door to door, as they were tasked with taking a census of Chinese residents. When they knocked on the door of what the *Morning Oregonian* described as a rambling tenement, they expected to find a family. When Sumata unbarred his door and unlocked the bolt, he expected customers. Sumata was disappointed, to say the least, when he saw the patrolmen at his door. It is possible that Sumata knew the two officers by sight; the previous year, an S. Sumata, who owned a restaurant on the same street, was busted by Miller and Wellbrook. At this restaurant, they found a bottle of sake and a quart of whiskey. Miller and Wellbrook were also well known in the North End for busting Chinese-run lotteries, fortune tellers and others for any crime they could pin on someone of Asian descent. The *Morning Oregonian* labeled them as the "Chinatown squad" in an article that read, "The regular Sunday raids on Chinatown by Sergeant Robson and Patrolmen Wellbrook and Miller, the Chinatown squad, netted 10 Chinese yesterday."

Sumata responded to the unwanted guests by trying to close the door as quickly as he could. The two patrolmen were quicker, and the two stopped

An early panoramic photo of Portland and its waterfront. *Courtesy of Library of Congress.*

the door from shutting. The two officers then entered, finding an elaborate sake-distilling plant. There were two stills in operation over a gas stove, one with a five-gallon capacity and the other with a ten-gallon capacity. There were seventeen fifty-five-gallon barrels of a mash made from rice and water located in another room. They found plenty of finished product, as well: nearly thirty gallons of sake that had been colored with liquid caramel to make the product look more like whiskey. Most moonshine operations move the liquor from the distillery as soon as it is made. It is less of a crime to be caught with a still than to be caught with a bunch of illegal booze.

After seeing the operation, Officer Wellbrook, said "Well, you're under arrest, old man." According to the officers, Sumata panicked at the thought of being busted. He allegedly threatened to kill himself and then ran into another room to try to find a weapon to carry out the threat. With no weapon to be found, Sumata attempted to fight off the police, but realized that he was outnumbered and stopped. Then, in a calm manner, he asked the officers, "Alright, what are you going to do with me?" The *Morning Oregonian* teased that outcome in the subheading of an article: "Suicide Effort Spoiled."

The police hauled Sumata in and turned him in to revenue agents Littell, Mann and McGill. After a day in federal judge Wolverton's courtroom, Sumata would end up with a three-month sentence and a one hundred dollar fine. The headline for the article about his sentencing was titled "Japanese Moonshiner Sentenced."

CHAPTER 8

ALL IN THE FAMILY ON PETTYGROVE STREET

The first member of the Balich family to get in trouble with the dry laws was Mike. He lived at Sixteenth and Pettygrove in downtown Portland, Oregon, and ran a soft drink business on that same corner. When his establishment was raided in November 1917, the authorities found four quarts of whiskey. Mike pleaded guilty and was fined one hundred dollars.

The next Balich busted was Mike's wife, Antonia. She didn't respond as well to getting busted. During her arrest, she became violent. Deputy Sheriff Roy Kendall knocked on Balich's door because he had heard it was a place that was selling moonshine. Instead of Mike, he met Antonia. She was willing to make a deal with this man who was unknown to her. For the amount of booze he wanted, she gave him the price of thirty dollars. Sheriff Kendall told her, "Thirty dollars for that booze? That's too much, besides"—and instead of finishing his sentence, he opened his coat to show her his sheriff star, to which Antonia responded with a simple "Uh huh" before grabbing a butcher knife. During the ensuing struggle, Kendall got cuts on his hands and his chin, but he was able to subdue Antonia before she did any life-threatening damage. Kendall arrested Antonia and confiscated a gallon of corn whiskey for evidence. When the case went to court, all Antonia received as punishment was a one hundred dollar fine.

The next one hundred dollar fine the Balichs received came a few months later, when Mike tried to befriend a police officer. Police officer Wilson knocked on the Balichs' door and told Mike that he was sick and needed a drink. Mike knew Wilson was an officer because he had seen him bust a relative of his recently, but he thought this could be a way to gain the officer's trust, so he went down to his cellar, brought up a bottle of wine and gave it to the officer free of charge. The officer took the bottle and then showed Mike his thanks for the hospitality by arresting him. In court, Mike would be fined the now-familiar one hundred dollars. At this point, it must have just seemed like part of the cost of doing business. When Mike paid the fine, he was quoted as saying that he wouldn't offer a drink to another officer ever again, even if he should meet up with one in the Sahara Desert.

Around this time, Mike's brother John got arrested as well for violating the dry laws. At this time, John was partners with Mike in the soft drink business, and he also ran a pool hall in one of the storefronts of Sixteenth and Pettygrove. For what and with how much he was caught was not revealed, but the amount of the fine was reported as one hundred dollars.

For a while after this, the Balichs were cautious and didn't get caught, but there were other small busts nearby. Four months later, the police searched a suspicious pile of wood in front of the pool hall and found eight pints of moonshine whiskey. A grocery store on Seventeenth and Pettygrove, one block west of the Balichs' establishment, was busted for selling moonshine. The police had gotten suspicious of the long lines of people going in and out of the store. Jack Vidak, the store's proprietor, was arrested. He was sentenced to ten days and had to pay a $200 fine. The cost of business was going up. The next day, John Balich was busted again. If there was a connection to the Balichs and Vidak's store other than proximity, that information is lost to time.

Mike was a funny character. His Sahara Desert joke wasn't the only time he had a quip ready when he was in trouble. An amusing incident took place when he got raided and the police said that they found booze hidden in weird places. One pint was in a basket filled with streamers that had a toy duck on top hiding the bottle. Another bottle was found in a photo album on his dresser. He had cut a bottle-sized hole in each page so he could hide the bottle within. Only a couple of pages were left uncut; one had a photo of a woman. One of the officers asked him if it was a picture of his wife. Mike responded, "Nope. That's my mother-in-law. I kept her picture there because I thought she would frighten away bad luck."

The family's bad luck continued. In 1921, Mike and John lost their license to operate their soft drink business. John tried to file for other business licenses. He filed an application to open a secondhand store, but the commissioner stated that he had been in too much trouble to be trusted in business again.

A bird's-eye view of Portland circa 1903. *Courtesy of Library of Congress.*

In 1922, Antonia was busted once again. This time, she was caught operating a still outside of town. The authorities found 350 gallons of wine, 25 gallons of diluted alcohol, 14 gallons of mash and a 40-gallon-capacity still. Antonia was busted by four officers. One of them was Sheriff Kendall. It had been a couple of years since the night she cut him up, but I imagine it still tickled him to arrest her, especially catching her with the still and so much alcohol on hand.

Mike was busted in November with 100 gallons of wine and 50 gallons of mash at his home. After these busts, Antonia and Mike were rarely mentioned in the papers again. They must have given up on moonshining.

John was busted and fined many more times in the years that followed, even after Prohibition ended. He was busted twice in 1936; once, he got caught and tried to quickly pour the booze down the drain of a sink, but he didn't run water with it. The arresting officers pulled the gooseneck pipe where the liquid had pooled and took it with them as evidence. For this incident, John received a suspended six-month sentence, and that was the last mention of a Balich getting busted for selling booze: the end of an era.

CHAPTER 9

THE INFAMOUS ERICKSON DABBLES IN MOONSHINE

August "Gus" Erickson was much more than a moonshiner. He is a legendary figure in Portland history. His famous Erickson's Saloon building in downtown Portland has been built and rebuilt over the years, the most famous version being the one he had built in 1895.

One thing that Erickson's bar was known for was the actual bar itself. Erickson proclaimed it to be the "longest bar in the world" at 684 feet—though that number likely represents the total length of the five bars in the place, not one long, magnificent bar. Besides the legendary bar, Erickson also had a stage for concerts and a grand pipe organ that was supposedly worth $5,000.

According to an article by Stewart Holbrook for *Esquire*, Erickson's was a fancy bar with all the best fixtures and mirrors. When do you even see a bar with mirrors anymore? The ones in the bathrooms are already too much. No one wants to see themselves when they are sloshed. Some of our faces bloat, and some of us turn red. See any celebrity's DUI mugshot for an example of how poor one can look while intoxicated.

Through a few business failings that included bad deals, a fire, rumors of his alcoholism and the dry laws, Erickson ended up selling his legendary establishment. Before he sold that property, he was able to set himself up with a smaller operation called the Clackamas Tavern. This establishment was nice but not as grand as Erickson's Saloon. Whereas Erickson's was famous for its grandness, Clackamas Tavern was known for its "famous Chicken Dinners," or so it was claimed in an ad that ran in the *Big O Magazine* in 1915.

Erickson's Cafe and Concert Hall

THIRD STREET ENTRANCE

Above: Exterior of Erickson's Saloon. *Courtesy of City of Portland (OR) Archives, A2004-001.230.*

Right: The infamous August "Gus" Erickson. *Courtesy of City of Portland (OR) Archives, A2004-001.230.*

AUGUST ERICKSON
PROPRIETOR

As Oregon went dry, Erickson had no plan to change his business model. He may not have had his beautiful downtown Portland location or his world-famous large bar, but he still had an establishment where he sold booze. Now he just did it illegally, and it was of the moonshine variety. The location of the Clackamas Tavern was on the outskirts of Oregon City, near Carver and Baker's Bridge: a fitting spot, since the first moonshine bust in Oregon had happened in that city.

The biggest bust for Erickson happened in 1917. He might not have gotten caught at this point, except he got drunk one night and got abusive toward his wife. His abuse was loud enough to awaken the curiosity of his upstairs tenant, A. Sauvie. Sauvie questioned Erickson about what was going on downstairs. This inquiry into what Erickson probably considered his personal business angered him. The next thing Sauvie knew, Erickson turned his aggression toward him. He grabbed a big cleaver and then ran up the stairs after Sauvie. Sauvie made it inside his room before Erickson could strike him with the cleaver. Instead, Erickson chopped away at his door with the large cleaver until he made it inside.

Sauvie had few options for escape. One was past the man holding the cleaver, or he could go out the window. Sauvie decided on the window. He

The Clackamas Tavern, where you could go for the "famous chicken dinner" and moonshine. *Courtesy of the Clackamas County Historical Society.*

climbed out of it and made his way onto the roof; from there, he jumped down to the ground.

Now Erickson was furious. He went back downstairs and grabbed his .30-30 rifle. His wife then made the nearly fatal mistake of appearing on the stairs. Erickson saw her, pointed his rifle and took a shot. The bullet missed. Mrs. Erickson then ran up the stairs while he followed, shooting at her. In Erickson's drunken state, he had poor aim and missed her three more times but did shoot out two windows. Like Sauvie, Mrs. Erickson made her escape out a window. The window she climbed out of was adjacent to the fire escape, which made for an easy getaway. Once on the ground, she ran barefoot into an adjoining grove.

Since both people Erickson fired his gun at escaped, it wasn't long before the police were called. Mrs. Erickson was the first to get to a phone. Two officers showed up, Sheriff Wilson and Deputy Frost. During the time between his victims escaping and the police showing up, Erickson had set his gun down. When Erickson saw the two officers, he made a dash for his rifle. He had just picked it up when Sheriff Wilson yelled for him to stop and explained that he would be in real trouble if he didn't set the gun back down.

Erickson was arrested, but before they took him out of there, they discovered three partly filled whiskey bottles. Erickson told them he had manufactured the whiskey himself and that it was all he had on his property. The two officers didn't believe him, so Deputy Frost stayed behind to watch the tavern while Sheriff Wilson took Erickson in and then went about securing a search warrant.

When Sheriff Wilson returned, he brought a search warrant and Deputy District Attorney Burke with him. During their search, they found a hidden assortment of various liquors underneath a trap door that concealed a concrete tub three by five by six feet containing about sixty bottles of assorted whiskey. Elsewhere on Erickson's property, they found a still for making whiskey, as well as beer-making equipment. Along with all this contraband, they also found two slot machines in working order.

For Erickson's shenanigans that night, he was hit with four charges: assault with a deadly weapon, operating two nickel-in-the-slot machines, unlawfully having liquor in his possession and unlawfully manufacturing liquor. For these crimes, he received a seven-month jail sentence from Justice of the Peace John Sievers. A week later, Circuit Judge James Ulysses Campbell sentenced him to six months, to run concurrently with the previous sentence, and a $150 fine for conducting a nuisance. His wife also filed for divorce.

Judge James Ulysses Campbell.
Courtesy of the Clackamas County Historical Society.

Erickson was released early from the four charges but was hit with a fifth charge: assault with a deadly weapon. He pleaded guilty and received another six months but was immediately paroled because of his reported poor health.

This would all lead to the end of the Clackamas Tavern. Mrs. Erickson received the tavern in the divorce. She later sold it to a man whose plan was to turn it into his summer home.

Erickson's luck continued its downward trajectory. Two years later, he was in downtown Portland again, this time operating a soft drink shop. There, he was busted with six quarts of liquor. Most embarrassing for Erickson was that he could have been released from jail for the crime, but the once-wealthy man lacked the $150 he needed to pay his fine.

In 1923, Erickson was still operating his soft drink establishment, but this time, he had a scheme set up where you could buy booze, but you had to pay one person for it, then you were directed to go to a little room where it would be handed to you through a hole. This way, the money and the liquor were kept separate, so that one could get busted for having liquor but not the worse crime of selling liquor. This also kept the customers from being able to tell authorities who they received the booze from.

Prohibition agents had been watching Erickson's establishment and couldn't figure out who was distributing the liquor—that is, until Prohibition Agent J.F. Roy came up with a simple plan. He went up to the bar, paid Erickson for a drink and received directions of where to go. Then, when the hand came through the hole with the drink, he slapped a handcuff on it and slapped the other cuff onto something solid. With the booze distributor stuck, Officer Roy had the time to find his way to the other side of the hole, where he found Erickson struggling, trying to get his hand back. For this bust, Erickson lost his business license for six months.

After this probationary period, Erickson went back to breaking Prohibition with his new soda shop. It wasn't long before he was busted again, this time with nineteen pints of moonshine.

Prohibition-era Portland. *Author's collection.*

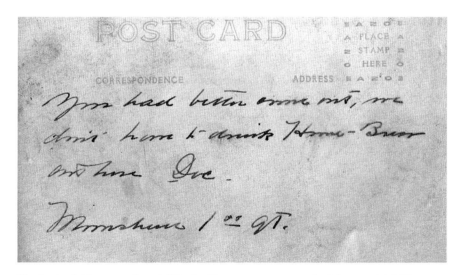

The back of this postcard read, "You had better come out, we don't have to drink Home-Brew out here. Moonshine 1.00 qt." *Author's collection.*

Erickson died in January 1925 at the Good Samaritan hospital; he was a prisoner at the time, convicted as a bootlegger. It's no wonder that the legend of August Erickson has held the interest of the people in the Pacific Northwest. It's a real riches-to-rags story. August Erickson was at one time a major success story; he operated a grand saloon, and he was a wealthy man. But through a combination of dry laws, bad decisions, bad behavior and bad luck, he died relatively poor and incarcerated.

PART IV

MOONSHINING TURNS DEADLY

CHAPTER 10

THREE DEAD IN PLAINVIEW

Every man who buys moonshine is guilty as hell. Every man who drinks the stuff is as much to blame as the bootlegger. There is a curse on every man who has anything to do with it. This is an orderly, law-abiding community, and here the damned hell-broth makes three widows as well as making orphans of Rev. Healy's little girl Eleanor and Sheriff Kendall's son Clark. It brings disgrace to us all.
—Unnamed member of the posse that went to the West homestead
after the shootings

This tragedy began when Sheriff Charles Kendall and Reverend Roy Healy showed up at the West property on June 21, 1922. They were looking for a rumored moonshine operation. According to the *Morning Oregonian*, Reverend Healy came along because he was working on a book about the enforcement of Prohibition.

Sheriff Charles Kendall was born in Chalfants, Ohio, in the late 1860s. Law enforcement had not always been his career path. Before coming to Oregon, he was a teacher at a business college in Cincinnati. He spent some time in Kansas, where he married Estella Scott in 1901. After their marriage, they tried living in California for three years but eventually found their way to Oregon. Kendall was elected sheriff in 1918.

The Reverend Roy Healy was younger than the sheriff. He was born in 1886 in Lebanon, Oregon, and educated at the Eugene Bible University. He was a born and raised Oregonian, but through his religious work, he spent time as a pastor in California as well as in Anacortes and Zillah,

Wyoming. At the time of the incident, he was pastor at the First Christian Church of Albany.

Dave West, the owner of the property and alleged moonshiner, was older than the other two. He was sixty-nine years old, born in 1854 in Hendricks County, Indiana. His wife's name was Ellen West, formerly Ellen DeAtley. She was also born in Indiana. Aside from the moonshining, Dave West was a bit of a farmer, a trapper and a hunter.

The West place was a forty-acre farm located on a private road about a mile northeast of Plainview, a small community about fourteen miles east of Albany. Dave West and his wife were not the only people at the farm that day. Myrtle DeAtley, Ellen's nephew's young wife, was there with her two children. The property consisted of a house, a barn and an old shed. The shed's original purpose was drying animal pelts. Then, for a bit, West used it as a chicken coop, but at the time of the visit from the sheriff and pastor, it was where he kept his moonshine operation.

When the two men arrived at the farm, they went right to the task at hand: locate the still, which they did. Once the still was located, they headed to the house to talk to the owner of the property. The house showed signs that a trapper lived there. There were five throws made from beaver and otter pelts. West did the trapping and tanning, and his wife did the finishing.

The three men had a conversation in the kitchen, during which the sheriff was overheard telling West that he'd better get ready to accompany them to Albany. West started to get mad when the sheriff questioned his wife, Ellen, and tried to get her to admit that she was hiding liquor in the house.

After this, West went out to the shed with the sheriff, who allegedly smashed the worm of the still with a hammer and told West that he was a crazy old fool for thinking he could get away with making moonshine. This disrespect made West furious, and he stormed back into the house. His wife saw him come in and could see he was upset. Later, she told Fred Lockley, a reporter from the *Oregon Daily Journal* that "he was high strung" and that "he was so deadly cool, I knew he was at white heat."

Fred Lockley was the reporter who interviewed Ben Jarrell, the King of the Moonshiners. He was a popular reporter, and Ellen felt comfortable talking to him. She told him,

> *Pretty soon my husband came in terribly excited and said he wasn't going to let anybody come on his place and destroy his property. You see the officers had seized traps once and had later given them back with an apology for having taken them.*

A lawman next to a captured still with a long "worm" in Columbia County. *Courtesy of Columbia County Museum Association.*

Dave was upset, and Ellen asked him not to grab his gun, but he did. Before he went back outside, he said, "What he is doing hurts me. I can't let him destroy my property and trample on my feelings." Dave then told his wife and Mrs. DeAtley to take the children inside. With that said, he took his rifle and headed out the back door, muttering; his wife thought he said something like, "It would be all right if they would come here like gentlemen, but they can't break things up."

Mrs. DeAtley took her two children from the backyard into the house, and then she heard a shot. That first shot went through Sheriff Kendall's back and pierced his heart. His death was likely instant. After hearing the shot, Mrs. DeAtley hurried the children upstairs. From the stairwell, she was able to see out the front of the house, and what she saw was Reverend Healy running toward the road. That is when she heard the second shot and saw Reverend Healy fall to the ground.

Once things calmed down, Mrs. DeAtley called to get her husband to come to the farm. When Harry DeAtley showed up, he saw the body of Reverend Healy. Harry addressed West with shock: "My god Uncle Dave, what have you done?" Harry then gathered his family in preparation to leave the farm. Before the DeAtleys left, West gave Harry instructions: "I want you to tell the coroner to come with a helper and get the bodies. I won't be taken alive. I will kill anyone who comes to get me."

When the DeAtleys arrived in Plainview, Harry called coroner F.C. Fisher and told him the whole story, including the threat. The authorities knew that West was a hunter and he had just killed two men, one of whom was armed, so the threat was taken seriously, and precautions were taken. The authorities devised a plan to gather up a posse and surround the whole farm before any attempts were made to capture Dave West. Ten armed men were selected. The leader of the posse was D.S. Smith, a former Linn County sheriff.

The men arrived at West's property at ten thirty that evening There was much fear that more blood would be shed before they were able to arrest or kill Dave West. Before searching the property on foot, they used a spotlight from a police vehicle to look for signs of West; they saw nothing. Then they put the car in neutral and pushed it into the yard. The automobile served two purposes: it provided the light with which to search, and if Dave West jumped out, they could hopefully use the vehicle as a shield for some protection in case it became a shootout.

West was located in the barn on his property, and when the authorities opened the door, the tension and fear of more violence came to an end, because inside was the lifeless body of Dave West, who, just like the other two men, had been killed by a single shot from a .30-30 Remington fired by West.

Mrs. West was at her son's house when she got the news. She told the authorities that West must have died sometime in the last hour and a half, as he had sent her away at nine. She was there with Dave for nearly six hours after the slayings. During that time, he milked a cow, fed a horse and did some other chores that needed doing.

While Dave did those chores, Mrs. West prepared dinner, but she would not eat. Dave encouraged her to, saying, "You have a hard time ahead and you will need to keep up your strength." She responded, "I will drink a cup of coffee. I can't swallow the food with those two dead men lying out by our house." During the meal, Dave told her, "This will be our last supper together. We have had our ups and downs but we have been happy together and you have been a good wife to me."

Three lives were lost that day in the fight against liquor, and it is unclear if West even sold the moonshine he made. Henry and Myrtle DeAtley wrote and signed a statement that said, "We wish to state that while Uncle Dave had made some liquor for his own use, he would not give any to anyone, except a personal friend, much less sell it to anyone."

The following summer, at the American Legion building, a movie premiered that was based on the incident, directed by W.J. Herwig, the superintendent of the Oregon Anti-Saloon League. The movie was titled *The Last Raid of Sheriff Kendall of Linn County*. Little is known about this lost film, but an ad for the movie in the *Bend Bulletin* read, "This picture depicts the last and fatal raid of a faithful officer of Oregon. The scenes were taken on the very spot where the tragedy occurred." This movie was taken around the country and shown at various community centers, churches and fraternal organizations. The last few public screenings of the movie were in Pennsylvania, the last publicized taking place in May 1931 at an unnamed Methodist church. If there is a print still in existence, it is probably in storage, in a church, collecting dust, somewhere in Pennsylvania.

CHAPTER 11

DEATH AND MOONSHINE IN GRAND RONDE

On September 2, 1922, a Friday, a dance was held in the newly built logging town of Grand Ronde. The previous year, International Harvester had laid out the townsite. Then, the Spaulding-Miami Lumber company set up a logging operation, which led to a rail line, new buildings and electricity.

The dance was going on that night with no issues, even though there was moonshine available if you knew who to talk to. Phillip Warren had moonshine available for two dollars. Warren was a thirty-one-year-old Native American. He was a husband and had seven children. When he was written about in the newspaper, if he was lucky, they called him an Indian. Many times, they referred to him as a "redskin." One opinion piece, because of his Native heritage, referred to him as a "man presumably of primitive instincts."

Unbeknownst to this local dealer of moonshine, if he was truly that, there were men of authority nearby: Prohibition officers Glen H. Price, Grover Todd, E.L. Marshall and Benton Kellen, as well as Tillamook County Deputy Sheriff E.W. Holden. With them was a man named Jasper Perry, who had recently been busted for an alleged violation of the Prohibition law. That evening, Jasper was tasked with finding and buying moonshine. Once that was done, the officers would bust the moonshiner. Later, during a trial, Jasper denied that he was promised immunity for helping the officers.

According to the original articles about this case, the night went like this: Jasper made his way into the dance and mixed in well. Before long,

Train tracks running through Grand Ronde. *Author's collection.*

he was able to find the moonshine he was looking for from Phillip Warren and Henry Petite. They made the deal for the liquor near a garage, and Prohibition officer Glen H. Price allegedly witnessed the two-dollar transaction between the men.

Glen H. Price was a veteran of World War I, where he was a first sergeant and was stationed at Camp Lewis. Once the war was over, he built a family with his wife, Nettie Mabel Price, who was twenty-one years old at that time. Together, they had three children. The oldest was three years old, and the other two were twins, a boy and a girl who were eight months old.

Price arrested Warren and Petite and put them in his Dodge automobile. Petite was the first one to jump over the side and make a break for it. Taking this as his cue, Warren made an escape attempt, as well. Price went after Warren and was able to overtake him; Warren fought to get away, and Price hit him in the head, leaving a wound above his eye. The blow to the head stopped Warren from struggling, and he was once again put into the automobile. Price then left Warren with Jasper Perry. Once Price was out of sight, Warren overpowered Perry, bailed from the automobile and ran away.

Why was Warren left with Perry? Where were the other officers? Benton Kellen was back at the hotel, resting. E.L. Marshall was said to be eating midnight supper at a local restaurant. Todd and Holden's excuse was that they had simply excused themselves from the party.

Marshall, who was at a restaurant eating dinner, was the first one to see Warren when he returned from his house with a .25-35 rifle. Warren walked into the restaurant where Marshall was eating his meal, pointed his rifle right at him and asked where the driver of that Dodge automobile was. Marshall's response was to ask, "What's the matter, someone run over you?" Warren's only response was, "They'll find out." When Marshall was questioned in the

Glen H. Price was stationed at Camp Lewis in Washington during World War I. *Author's collection.*

94

courtroom, he said that he really did think Phillip Warren had been in an automobile accident because he had so much blood on him. A woman who was closing her shop said that Warren had walked by and asked her if she knew where the men with the Dodge car were. In the trial, she said, "He was all covered in blood and excited."

During this time, Price, Holden and Todd made their way to where their Dodge automobile was parked. They were standing in such a way that when Warren was heading down the road toward them with his rifle, he could only see the car, not the men on the other side of it.

As Warren walked around the car, right before he would have seen the officers, Price jumped out and tried to grab the rifle. At only 135 pounds, Price was much smaller than Warren, who was described as being well built. During the struggle, the gun went off, firing a shot into a brick wall. The struggle ended when Price fell to the ground. Warren took this opportunity and shot Price twice, once in the stomach and once in the arm. The arm was the lethal shot; the bullet went into Price's arm and through his side and continued into his heart, killing him.

While this was happening, Holden opened fire but only got four shots out before his gun jammed. One of the bullets hit Warren in the hip.

Officer Grover Todd, who was forty-one years old and had a wife and four children at home, tried to make his escape. He dropped to the ground and attempted to crawl away out the other side of the car, but Warren made his way in that direction and shot him in the head. The *Morning Oregonian* wrote that "practically the whole side of Todd's head was blown away." The bullet had gone through Todd's skull and out through his right eye. Todd lost consciousness and died an hour later. He had only been working as a revenue agent for a few months when it proved to be a fatal career move.

Phillip Warren limped away from the scene; nobody dared to follow.

Phillip Warren's father, John Warren, had heard about the shooting and was driving around looking for him. When he saw his wounded son, he picked him up and drove him home, where Phillip lived with his mother, father, wife and seven children. After dropping off his son, he went in search of a doctor—whom he found back at the scene of the crime.

Dr. Russell had already arrived on the scene and declared the two officers dead. John Warren approached the doctor, who was looking over the two dead men his son had killed. John asked Dr. Russell to take care of his son, who was wounded at his home. Dr. Russell went to the Warren home to care for the wounded man. While he was there, Sheriff Orr showed up.

Sheriff Orr had been notified by O.P. Chase about the double murders. The sheriff drove as fast as he could from Dallas to Grand Ronde, a twenty-mile trip. Once he arrived, he asked John Warren to come out.

John Warren and the sheriff, it was said, knew each other well. The two talked about the surrender of Phillip. John agreed with the sheriff that there had been too much bloodshed already. Plus, Phillip had no more fight left in him; he, too, had shed much of his own blood that night and had little energy left.

Sheriff Orr and O.P. Chase entered the house behind John. Both officers had their guns drawn, just in case. Phillip Warren was lying on a bed with a hole in his thigh. He didn't resist arrest and was glad that Orr was the one to come arrest him, since he knew him well.

On the way to the hospital in Dallas, Warren told Orr that "they beat me up and I got them for it" and said that if the officers had just arrested him without beating on him, he would have started no trouble.

Phillip Warren was potentially in big trouble. Federal District Attorney Humphreys told the press that since the violence was toward federal agents in the discharge of government duties, it was possible that if Warren was found guilty of first-degree murder, he could be hanged.

When Phillip Warren was arraigned in front of Judge Harry H. Belt of Polk County, he pleaded not guilty. There would be two separate trials, one for each of the deceased. The first trial date was set for October 9. The trial would focus on the murder of Grover Todd.

Lester Humphreys was appointed federal district attorney in 1919. *Courtesy of Lori Terwilliger.*

The prosecution included District Attorney Helgerson and Walter L. Tooze Jr. Tooze had offered to assist free of charge after hearing of the crime. The prosecution was also offered any assistance needed from Federal District Attorney Lester Humphreys. Helgerson said that he was considering the offer.

The trial took place the following month in Dallas, Oregon. When the trial came, the headline in the *Morning Oregonian* was "Trial of Red Man for Murder Begun." To get to twelve members of the jury, they went through a pool of sixty-one candidates. The potential jurors were all asked if they believed in the death penalty. Nine of them did not, so they were excused. Others were excused because they already had opinions on the case. Most members of the jury were farmers, and their names were Henry McElmurry, G.F. Brown, J.W. Childers, Gus Lake, Henry Gage, W.D. Grosline, A.V. Oliver, W.L. Murphy, B.I. Ferguson, T.J. Gardner, J.P. Hamilton and J.E. Mason.

The first witness called by the state at the trial was Jasper Perry. Some people called him a stool pigeon for setting up Phillip Warren. During Perry's questioning, he denied that he was promised immunity for his own run-in with bootlegging. Perry told his version of the story, and the officers corroborated this version.

Dr. Russell was called to the stand; he was there to testify about the condition of Grover Todd's body when he examined it at the scene of the crime and proclaimed him dead. Dr. Russell was cross-examined by Warren's council, Oscar Hayter. Hayter asked Dr. Russell about the blow to the head that Warren received that night. Dr. Russell agreed that it might have been such a harsh blow that it confused his thinking.

The state concluded its case, and now it was the defense's turn. The defense called many witnesses, including Henry Petite, the man Warren was arrested with, and Warren's mother, father and sister.

One witness testified that at least one of the two slain men had been drinking that night. When Jasper was questioned about this, he confirmed that Glen Price had been drinking liquor out of a small beer bottle, but he claimed that the bottle was still half full after the shooting.

Henry Petite, the other man who was arrested, testified that they met Jasper at the pool hall and Jasper invited them out to have a drink. Petite went on to say that all three of them—Warren, Jasper and himself—drank from a bottle that Jasper had. Petite said that they didn't know the other men were lawmen; even when they escaped, he claimed, they didn't know the other men were officers.

Other details of a different version of the narrative given during the trial were that Glen Price had brought booze to town with him, which he obtained from Tillamook, and that he brought it out to drink with Henry Petite and Phillip Warren. When they finished the booze Price had brought, Price asked Warren if he could obtain some more. Warren told him that he didn't know where to find any, but he did ask around and finally found a little bit of booze. After securing the alcohol, Price tried to arrest him.

The public didn't like these underhanded methods, and there was speculation that this would make the first-degree murder charge less likely. In the October 14 issue of the *Capital Journal*, an opinion piece on the case was published. Here is a brief excerpt that expressed the opinion of much of the public at that time:

The system followed by the slain officers was customarily used by special dry officers seeking victims in order to make a record of arrests. Coercion, intimidation and corruption were the methods employed, and as no booze was handy, the officers supplied it. For the ensuing shooting affray, they were as much to blame as anyone.

Throughout the trial, the jurors were not sure there was any evidence that Warren was the one who shot Todd. Since several men were shooting, the jurors thought it possible that Todd was hit by one of the other officers' bullets. Because of this, the members of the jury struggled to agree on the charge. At one point, they were at seven for murder in the second degree and five for manslaughter. After spending all night and day on their decision, they found Warren not guilty of the death of Glover Todd.

The second trial for Phillip Warren was set for January 11; this would be the trial for the murder of Glen H. Price, described as the weaker of the two cases. For this second trial, Warren kept the same attorney, Oscar Hayter. The state had the same council as the previous trial as well, Joseph Helgerson, assisted by Walter L. Tooze. The judge was Harry H. Belt.

Public opinion was on Phillip Warren's side. An unknown correspondent wrote this during the second trial:

Inconspicuously dressed in a brown, ready-made suit, Warren sat quietly this morning as counsel for the state and the defense led prospective jurors through the monotonous questioning to determine their qualifications to sit on the case. As he walked upstairs in company with a deputy sheriff, Warren was accosted by well-wishers who shook his hand, and to whose advantage he returned thanks in an almost timid manner. In Warren's face is seen none of the hardness commonly associated with the criminal.

The defense also had in its favor the perceived poor character of the officers, who, it was believed, had broken the law in their pursuit of Warren.

The prosecution had on its side two witnesses who claimed they had heard Phillip Warren threaten the lives of the two men. Plus, the prosecution would be introducing, with the help of Robert Craddock, a Portland police detective, evidence that the metal fragments they pulled from Glenn Price matched the type of bullet from a .25-35 rifle, the type of gun Warren had.

Warren was put on the stand during the trial, during which he claimed self-defense because he said that he believed Price was the one who shot him. When he was asked again about the selling of liquor, he told the court that he had not sold them liquor and that Price and Perry had offered him a drink on four different occasions. Sheriff Orr testified that he could smell liquor on Perry's breath that night.

The prosecution closed the state's case with a summary. When it was the defense team's turn, they must have figured that they already had this case won, because they said they "would waive argument."

With that, the court was closed, and the decision was left to the jury. The jury deliberated for over thirty hours before returning with its decision. Phillip Warren was again found not guilty.

Warren was released immediately, but there was no celebration for him, because it was said that he was heading straight home to his family, where his three-year-old son, Phillip Warren Jr., was ill with influenza and it was thought that he might not make it.

Regardless of the decisions of the court, Phillip Warren would be known as a murderer and a bootlegger. In government records, the official story is written as follows:

> *Agent Price, accompanied by Prohibition Agent Grover C. Todd attempted to take in custody one Phillip Warren, an Indian bootlegger in New Grande Ronde, Oregon. Warren escaped from the officers, obtained a rifle and fired, killing both Agents Price and Todd. He was taken in custody by the state authorities on the charge of murder.*

No mention of the officers plying Warren with liquor, no mention of them beating on him or the fact that he wasn't really a bootlegger until they made him one. No mention that he was found not guilty on all counts.

CHAPTER 12

THIS SHOT WILL KILL YOU

One of the earliest moonshine deaths in Oregon happened in December 1919. An article in the *Oregon Daily Journal* stated that a man from Seattle died in Portland; the moonshine turned out to be wood alcohol. Wood alcohol is methanol, an alcohol that is potent and lethal; while it will get you drunk, it also can lead to blindness, respiratory paralysis and even death. Methanol was and is still used in many products. It is used to make plastics, paints and even as fuel. An interesting note about this incident is that no names are given—which makes one wonder if it actually happened.

Another unnamed out-of-towner who supposedly died of drinking moonshine was mentioned in the papers, as well. The article was short but less than sweet. All it said was, "A seaman came to Portland thirsty. He drank moonshine in a north-end establishment. He is dead."

An additional unnamed man was written about in the *East Oregonian*. This story was the same as the previous one: no name and only a few lines. "When a Clatskanie laborer died after drinking some moonshine his body turned black. He wanted something with a kick in it and he got it."

People didn't just die from wood alcohol. Most of what was considered "rotten" moonshine was alcohol made using unsafe materials. Ben Jarrell, the King of the Moonshiners, expressed his opinion on moonshine in the Pacific Northwest during an interview with Fred Lockley for the *Oregon Daily Journal*. Here is the complete quote:

The people here in Oregon and Washington that are making mountain dew, don't know how to make it. In all my life I never made a drop of whiskey that was impure or adulterated. The only way to make whiskey right is to use nothing but copper in the still. When you use iron or galvanized iron for the worm you are sure to make very dangerous and harmful liquor. It is a slow poison. If I were a judge and a moonshiner were brought before me that used the kind of still they are using here in Oregon, I would send him up for life to protect the public. The moonshiners out here are giving moonshine liquor a bad name, and they deserve to be put out of business.

A similar article ran a month later in the *Oregon Sunday Journal*. This time, the interviewees were Johnson Smith, the federal Prohibition director, and Jesse Flanders, a Prohibition agent. They confirmed what Ben Jarrell had been saying, that many stills operating in Oregon were not made using copper. They were constructed using unsafe materials like wash boilers, kettles and galvanized containers. Smith and Flanders even suggested that some moonshine was tainted with lead. In an unattributed quote, one of them stated that "present moonshine is often a mixture of colored water, lead poisoning, and a nerve-deadening drug."

Things must have improved over time, because two years later, in 1922, Jesse Flanders was interviewed again, and he stated that the quality of moonshine was getting better and the chances of paralysis, blindness

Two men appear to be enjoying their drinks. *Courtesy of Willamette Falls & Landings Heritage Area Coalition & Old Oregon Photos.*

Wood engraving by John Warner Barber, made in 1872 to show the ill effects that alcohol had on society. *Courtesy of Library of Congress.*

or instant death from overindulgence were decreasing. Flanders said, "Chemical tests show that the poisonous liquors of a few years ago are disappearing and a better grade of moonshine is being produced."

This might have been true, but the Anti-Saloon League kept pushing the story that all moonshine was of poor quality. In their press release for the movie they produced called *The Last Raid of Sheriff Kendall of Linn County*, they wrote this about the quality of moonshine: "The poisonous conditions under which moonshine is manufactured is shown by stills and coils covered with verdigris. It is said that men who have been drinking moonshine whiskey, after seeing this picture have sworn off forever." Verdigris is a bluish-green patina that forms on copper or brass when it oxidizes.

These deaths, if real, were tragic, but the most tragic stories are of the younger people affected by real rotgut whiskey. Eighteen is much too young of age to pass in the pursuit of getting a buzz.

TRUE ROTGUT WHISKEY

In 1925, three young men pooled their money to buy moonshine in Pilot Rock, Oregon. The cost was eleven dollars for a gallon. William Sprague and Chester Michael were eighteen years old, but their younger buddy, Cecil Wagner, was the one who knew how to get the liquor. The young men allegedly bought it from a moonshiner supposedly named Jim Best. Not much is known about Jim Best, if he did exist, because there are no other known references to that name during that period in Umatilla County—or in any parts of Oregon, for that matter.

William Sprague must have been the only one of the three who could handle the rotten taste of Jim Best's moonshine, because he was the only one who drank enough to get sick.

A postcard showing the first train to arrive in Pilot Rock. *Author's collection.*

Local Pilot Rock doctor W.G. Oliver claimed that he tended to the boy during two attacks he had that were blamed on the tainted 'shine. The doctor didn't elaborate on the symptoms of the attacks.

Then, on March 21, 1925, poor William died. Because of his young age, the death was looked at as suspicious, so an inquest was made into his death. An autopsy was performed by Dr. E.O. Parker, and it was found that much of the mucous membrane of William's stomach had been eaten away. To the coroner and Dr. Oliver, this indicated that the young man had consumed a large amount of poison. Dr. E.O. Parker said that this was the third time he had seen a death caused by moonshine in this way.

ONE BOY IS STRICKEN BLIND, ANOTHER HAS A CASE OF THE JAKE LEG

Another, less deadly, tragedy involving moonshine and a couple of youths happened in April 1929. One boy went blind, while another boy suffered from temporary paralysis.

The two boys were dancing at the Mellow Moon dance hall and skating rink in West Salem. From whom they obtained the alcohol is unclear. When asked after the incident, one boy claimed that the man was a heavyset fat man, while the other described him as tall and slender with a mustache. This made it impossible to find a suspect. The police believed the boys were either protecting someone or had made the tainted liquor themselves. From their symptoms, it sounds like the two drank from two different bottles.

Elmer "Pickles" Lenon was taken home from the dance because he was complaining of pains. Before he got home, the illicit booze caused the left side of his body to go into a state of paralysis. He couldn't use his left leg. This was not an uncommon reaction during Prohibition; it was usually from someone passing off Jamaica ginger extract as booze. This extract did have a high alcohol content, anywhere from 70 to 90 percent. It wasn't the extract that caused the paralysis; it was the additive that was required during Prohibition to keep people from drinking it, which was called tri-ortho-cresyl phosphate. The effect was common enough that there was a slang term for the paralysis of one's legs that came from drinking the stuff. It was called "jake leg," and songs were even written about it at the time. There were "Jake Leg Blues," "Jake Walk Papa" and "Got the Jake Leg Too"—just to name a few.

Eddie Pickard experienced a different effect from the illegal booze. While dancing, his vision started getting blurry, and he eventually lost his eyesight completely. This was most likely caused by methanol in the moonshine, due to either poor distilling or adding wood alcohol to make the product more potent. The loss of eyesight was so severe that poor Eddie allegedly couldn't even see the light from a flashlight when it was shone in his eyes to test his vision.

Luckily for the two boys, their suffering was temporary. Within a day or two, both were back to normal.

The Death of a Young Man from Maupin

Fred Martin, a young man of twenty-three from Maupin, Oregon, was not so lucky—if booze is, in fact, to blame. When his death was first announced in the papers, it was blamed on a brief illness that the family believed to be spinal meningitis. According to the *Oregon Daily Journal*, Martin had been completely paralyzed leading up to his death. His funeral was only a few days later at Kelly Cemetery.

Four days after his death, an article titled "Citizens of Maupin, Suspecting Poison, Want Body Exhumed" ran in the *Oregon Daily Journal*. The townspeople theorized that the young man died from bad moonshine, and they made a request to coroner Burget to exhume the body for an inquest. Adding some weight to this theory was Dr. J.L. Elwood, who stated he was convinced that Martin's death was due to poisoning and demanded the county investigate the case.

An article that ran the next day in the *Sunday Oregonian* revealed that Martin had been drinking with friends before his death.

Fred Martin was a popular young man, and residents were upset about his death. Some even threatened violence against Earl Brazee, the man who sold him the liquor.

Fred Martin's body was never exhumed. Earl Brazee was arrested by Sheriff Chrisman but only ended up with a $250 fine when all was said and done, and that was just for the manufacture of intoxicating liquor.

Not So Deadly

Moonshine was deadly and dangerous all over the country, but in Oregon, at least, there doesn't seem to be a high death toll. There is a story here and there of one person dying but no mass deaths. A couple of quotes from

William S. Levens, the state Prohibition commissioner in 1926, sum up the situation. "It is said that moonshine is killing off many men. It is true that moonshine certainly is capable of killing a man. But it is interesting to look up statistics on the matter. These reveal that in the last year the saloons were open, there were more deaths from alcohol than in any year since prohibition has set in," Levens said. "The old whiskey was not so harmful as moonshine, but there were so many more drinking it that the death rate was larger."

CHAPTER 13

TWO DEAD MOONSHINERS AND AN EXPLODING APARTMENT IN BEND

T he year 1926 was a violent and explosive one for state Prohibition officer Clarendon McBride. In that year, he was involved in two different busts that resulted in the death of a moonshiner. He was also hit with a lawsuit from a man he arrested who claimed that McBride broke his hands during the arrest. Those events alone would mean an extreme year for anybody, but it gets worse from there; McBride also had the Bear Creek Gang try to end his life by blowing up an apartment complex they believed he lived in.

Clarendon Crawford McBride was born in 1897 in the little Oregon town of Eddyville, located in Lincoln County. When he was a young man, he and his brother would sometimes make extra money by peeling cascara bark. Peeling cascara was a popular way to earn money for youth at that time, because it could be sold to pharmaceutical manufacturers to make laxatives. Some people even made tea out of it, and there was a cute little rhyme about the benefits of cascara tea: "Mary had a little watch, she swallowed it one day and now she drinks cascara tea to pass the time away." McBride went to Oregon Agricultural College; later, that school was renamed Oregon State, and today it is known as Oregon State University. McBride had three years of education at that school before becoming a Prohibition officer like his older brother, Lawrence McBride. His plan was to get a job and make money to finance his final year of college.

The first incident involving McBride in 1926 that got him into legal trouble was in January, when he and A.F. "Buck" Mariott went to arrest restaurateur W.N. Egbert. Egbert claimed that McBride was rough with him and broke his hands. He would later sue for $5,000.

THE VAYLE TAYLOR INCIDENT

In February, Mariott, McBride and a man named Fern Lowell headed to the west slopes of Bear Creek, in Crook County near the border of Deschutes County. They didn't know that this moonshine bust would lead to a dead man and the eventual bombing of the Congress Apartments in Bend, Oregon.

Mariott, McBride and Lowell arrived at about three o'clock in the afternoon, but nobody was there. The three men removed a window from a door that led to the dugout where the moonshine operation was. Inside, they found ten barrels of mash brewing. Only one quart of finished moonshine would be found on the property. They waited for over eighteen hours for the owner of the still to show up. During that time, they put the glass back on the door so that the moonshiner wouldn't notice the disturbance.

At nine thirty the next morning, twenty-five-year-old Vayle Taylor arrived. Taylor was a much-beloved young man. He was born in Missoula in 1901. The first reference to Taylor in Oregon was in 1911, when his name was listed in the *Bend Bulletin* alongside others who had not been late or missed any days of school. In 1920, Taylor's mother passed. As a young adult, he worked on local farms, where he helped drive cattle and seed alfalfa.

The officers must have left some clue of their presence that caught Taylor's eye when he arrived home, because he grabbed a two-by-four that was about twelve feet long and placed it against the door that the officers were hiding behind.

The officers yelled out that he was under arrest, but Taylor didn't acknowledge their calls. He just walked away from the trapped officers and checked on the rest of his operation. Seeing nothing else out of the ordinary, he walked back to the door that the men were imprisoned behind. The glass window in the door was blackened by smoke, so Taylor lit a match and held it against the glass to illuminate the room behind it. It's possible that the men hid and he didn't see them, because the next thing Taylor did was remove the board and reach into the room. McBride took this opportunity to grab Taylor's arm and once again told him he was under arrest. Taylor struggled and was able to break free from McBride's strong grip. He then pushed the door shut and once again jammed the board against the door, blocking their way out.

McBride and Mariott had their weapons drawn as they slammed themselves against the door with their shoulders. They were successful in breaking the flimsy door, but as they did so, McBride's .38 automatic pistol went off. McBride would always claim that it was an accident, but the outcome was the same regardless. The bullet struck Taylor in the left side of his neck, breaking it. Vayle Taylor's body fell on the board he was using to hold the door shut. McBride, Mariott and Lowell attempted first aid, but it was futile; the young man had passed.

McBride and Lowell stayed at the scene, while Mariott took off for Millican to telephone both the Crook County and Deschutes officials. While Mariott was gone, McBride and Lowell made a fire to keep warm on a ridge to the west of the moonshine operation.

The first officers didn't arrive until just after three o'clock in the afternoon. They were the officers from Deschutes: Sheriff S.E. Roberts, Deputy Sheriff George Stokoe and District Attorney A.J. Moore.

As they awaited the arrival of the Crook County officials, some locals showed up, and they were not too pleased. Vayle Taylor was well known in his community, and many people were fond of him. One of the locals, after looking at McBride and Lowell in their sullen state, said "They're like licked dogs—they can't look you in the eye."

Sheriff Yancey, Coroner P.B. Poindexter and Dr. J.H. Rosenberg of Crook County showed up around five o'clock that evening. When they arrived, McBride wordlessly walked over to Sheriff Yancey and gave him his revolver. McBride was in terrible spirits, and he was described as broken by the incident. According to the *Bend Bulletin*, he kept repeating to his fellow officers that he would not have shot Taylor intentionally even if his own life was at stake. McBride would shoot and kill another man before the year was through.

P.B. Poindexter tried to get a coroner's inquest together at the scene using the locals that showed up as the jury, but it turned out that many of them were friends of Taylor and expressed their ill feelings toward the officers. One man said, "If the Bear Creek gang was here, the inquest would be held on the ground." A county official responded to that threat by saying, "Bring on the Bear Creek gang." After everyone calmed down, Poindexter declared that he would hold the inquest in Prineville.

The body of Vayle Taylor was strapped across a saddle on a horse borrowed from Mr. Ewing, who lived nearby and with whom Taylor had lived for several years. Later, when the body was searched, $190 was found; it was noted that one of the bills was a fifty. Taylor also had on a gold watch, and in one of his pockets was a letter he had planned to send to his father.

Before everyone left the scene, the still had to be taken care of. The county officials, along with McBride, Mariott and Lowell, broke up the two moonshine stills that were on the property. Then the stills were dragged, along with some boards and barrels, into the dugout. Then it was all set on fire.

With that done, the men, with Taylor's dead body strapped to Ewing's horse, made their way to their vehicles, while the remains of the still burned and the smoke filled the Bear Creek valley.

They arrived in Bend at seven o'clock that evening, and one of Sheriff Robert's first tasks was the displeasure of sending a telegram to Walter Taylor, Vayle's father, to inform him of his son's death.

It wasn't long after the incident that locals claimed it to have been an unjust killing. Some went as far as trying to justify Taylor's trapping the officers by saying that he had an inclination for playing practical jokes.

Poindexter's inquest was held in Prineville the following day with a jury of locals from that area. The witnesses called were Dr. J.H. Rosenberg, Sheriff Steve Yancey, A.F. Mariott, Clarendon McBride and Fern Lowell—all people on the state's side. The verdict: Taylor came to his death as the result of an accidental shooting. The record stated, "Complete exoneration for state Prohibition officer CC McBride and all others who might be involved with him in the fatal shooting of 25-year-old Vayle Taylor."

After McBride was exonerated, the local ranchers put up money to hire Boylan and Ramsey, two attorneys from Bend, to investigate the incident. The attorneys told the papers that they accepted the job strictly on a monetary basis, as they had no desire to be seen as criticizing the officers who investigated the death. Not much ever seemed to come out of their investigation.

THE EXPLOSION

The next big event in McBride's life happened in early March, less than a month after the Vayle Taylor incident. It took place in Bend, at the Congress Apartments, where A.F. Mariott was living with his wife. McBride sometimes took meals with the Mariotts, so the people who were out to get McBride after the Vayle Taylor incident thought he lived there.

The Congress Apartments were built two years previously, in 1924, as a single-story, five-unit complex in the Craftsman style. Before the incident, each unit was a studio setup with a built-in hide-a-bed cabinet.

It was around two thirty in the morning when the trouble started. At least, that is when people later remembered hearing Blaine barking. Blaine was a dog owned by a neighbor, John Payne; he was described as brown and part bulldog. Some of the locals thought that maybe if Blaine hadn't

It's surprising that it was possible to rebuild the Congress Apartments, with so much damage done to them. *Courtesy of Deschutes County Historical Society.*

been barking, the criminals would have spent more time preparing their attack. The goal was to blow up the Congress apartments to kill Clarendon McBride. Since McBride didn't live there, that goal would not have been realized, regardless of the time the criminals took.

The explosives were placed at the rear of the building, near the back of apartment 5, where A.F. Mariott and his wife were sleeping. The explosion wiped out a whole wall of unit 5. It took out all the partitions in the basement, as well. According to reports, fragments from the building were hurled through various walls of the other units at the speed of cannonballs.

Miss Alice Bush, a telephone operator who lived in one of the other units, had debris fall on her from the explosion, and even her bathtub was torn from its place. Alice had to be carried out by rescuers, as she was temporarily paralyzed from the waist down. She was the most injured in the incident. A.F. Mariott and his wife, whose apartment was the target of the attack, were physically unharmed.

A big chunk of wood from the building smashed through a neighboring house, as well. This house was occupied by R.H. Mansfield, a night watchman at the Brooks-Scanlon plant. The timber burst through the walls and fell just in front of the bed of his sleeping daughter. It was written in the *Bend Bulletin* that Mansfield's coworkers were going to raise money for his repairs.

The only clues to who set the explosion were the threats made to McBride about the Bear Creek Gang and the fact that someone had seen two men get

Another view of the wreckage. *Courtesy of Deschutes County Historical Society.*

into an automobile right after the explosion. A witness claimed that one of them had said, "It wasn't as loud as I thought it would be." Then they drove off toward Greenwood Avenue, never to be seen again.

It wasn't long before a crowd had gathered around the site of the explosion. At first, just the residents of the apartments and then all the surrounding neighbors showed up, still in their nightclothes, most wearing slippers and bathrobes. Before long, the press arrived. A reporter for the *Bend Bulletin* was on the scene within ten minutes of the explosion, a fact that the *Bend's* editors bragged about in the extra edition of the paper that they rushed to get out that morning—reminding their readers about the great service the paper provided.

Once officials arrived, Mariott and his wife were taken downtown. This would be a long day for Mariott, as he and McBride also had a court appointment regarding the restaurateur who claimed McBride broke his hands back in January.

Two people came out to investigate the explosion: one was a contractor named A.B. Taylor, and the other was an explosives expert named R.B. Cross. Taylor believed that whoever set the explosion probably used fifty or so sticks of number 2 TNT, while Cross believed that the culprit was an amateur because he saw residue that appeared to be spread out, which is not ideal for an explosion. For an explosion, you want everything tight, so that all the energy gets expelled at once, causing the most damage.

Later that day, McBride and Mariot would sit in a full courtroom for the case against them by Egbert for allegedly breaking his hands and causing him loss of business. The courtroom was full because of the interest in the officers from both the Vayle Taylor shooting and now the explosion. The case would go on for two days. One witness was a waitress who worked at Egbert's establishment. She claimed that she noticed no difference in the amount of clientele that visited the restaurant before and after the incident. During the trial, it was also revealed that Egbert's hand was broken previously when he got into a brawl with a former employee a few weeks before. One interesting fact of note was that Egbert was represented by one of the lawyers the locals had hired to investigate the Vayle Taylor incident. The case ended in McBride and Mariot's favor.

The culprits who set the explosion at the Congress Apartments were never caught, even though a $750 reward for information was offered by the Deschutes County Court.

ANOTHER MOONSHINER DEAD

McBride was involved in one more deadly incident in 1926. It took place in June, and it centered on another illegal liquor operation. McBride was trying to bust William Brown, who was an alleged moonshiner. Brown was also a husband and the operator of a store in Broadacres.

This incident took place further northwest than McBride's usual stomping ground. Broadacres is located between Salem and Woodburn. Another change was that McBride was working with a new group of officers. It's possible that after the broken hand incident, the killing of Vayle Taylor and the explosion at the Congress Apartments, it was decided that A.F. Mariott and McBride should dissolve their partnership and that McBride should move locales. The officers who joined him on this bust were C.B. Hill, R.D. Carter, E. Oaks and Claude Hickman.

To bust the moonshiner, McBride was trying to catch him in the act of selling. The authorities had suspected Brown for months. McBride had been talking to Brown for the last couple of days and was finally able to get a deal set up to buy sixty-three gallons of 'shine from him. Once the deal was done, McBride arrested and handcuffed Brown as his fellow officers listened from their hiding places on the property. As he was being arrested, Brown turned and yelled something in Greek in the direction of a barn.

In that barn were three armed men. According to the *Oregon Statesman*, they started shooting immediately after the yell. McBride responded to the shots by running toward the barn, firing as he went. John Kaboris was the first one to step out of the barn, rifle in hand. McBride shot him in the chest and the arm. Kaboris died almost immediately.

McBride's backup officers then jumped into action, but by the time they arrived at the barn, the other two armed men were gone, leaving only a pool of blood behind. One of them had been shot in the leg.

The two moonshiners had run from the barn to the house; they told the women who were inside that they were going to bury their guns. After that, they left the house.

After an exhaustive search for the two men, the officers focused their energy on trying to locate the moonshine still. The still was not found, but in the barn, they did find a heavy truck that was outfitted for the transportation of moonshine.

The following day, another search was conducted on the Brown farm, this time by the state Prohibition director, William Levens. The searchers found forty gallons of moonshine in a shed, but no still was located.

There was a rumor that James Angelus, the one who left the blood trail, had been seen ten miles away in the St. Paul neighborhood. This was unlikely in his condition and was proven untrue when he was located in a house a mere half mile away. His leg was in bad condition, and he was unable to put weight on it. He was taken to the hospital, where he had to be carried in.

Just like in the Vayle Taylor case, an inquest was held. Many witnesses were called: officers, ranchers and even the women that were in Brown's house at the time of the incident.

The women were seasonal workers from Washington, hired by William Brown to pick cherries; they claimed no knowledge of the liquor operation. During their testimony, they said that they estimated there were approximately thirty shots fired.

After hearing all evidence, a coroner's jury once again absolved McBride in a shooting. The verdict read, "We find that John Kaboris died as the result of a gunshot wound which penetrated his left chest and passed through his body. Such a wound was inflicted by C.C McBride, state Prohibition officer, in the performance of his official duties and under such circumstances as would constitute justifiable homicide."

It's possible that this incident was enough for McBride to get out of the law enforcement game, or if he did stay in, he had a much lower profile, because there isn't much more written about his law enforcement career. His obituary from his death in 1963 doesn't even mention this dark period of his life.

CHAPTER 14

THE MURDEROUS RAY SUTHERLAND OF LANE COUNTY

Ray Sutherland, King Killer of the Mountain—at least that's what they called him in the lead story of issue 39 of *Crime Does Not Pay*.

Crime Does Not Pay was a popular true-crime comic, first published in 1942, featuring a narrator named Mr. Crime who wears a white sheet and a white hat with the word *crime* on it. Mr. Crime sets up the stories similar to what EC Comics did a few years later with its horror hosts the Crypt Keeper, the Vault Keeper and the Old Witch.

In this comic, adapted from a "true story" by Dick Wood, Ray is portrayed as a man who is unhappy with his lot in life. He believes he is the smartest guy in the whole valley and deserves more. According to the *Oregonian*, he was "bent and bothered by ill health"; the *Eugene Register* described him as "six feet, one inch tall, slender and stooped. His arms are long and when walking [he] has a habit of drooping his arms slightly ahead of his body." The *Register* went on to describe his general appearance as "description tallies with that of the typical dime novel mountaineer villain."

In the comic version, for reasons that aren't made clear, Ray blames the deputies and sheriffs for his problems. Mr. Crime uses this to will him into action. The comic further exaggerates the story by adding armed robbery and even a train wreck involving a car full of women. But that does not mean the real story isn't exciting. This story has three separate incidents in which guns are fired and somebody is left dead.

Left: Splash page of the comic *Crime Does Not Pay*, with Mr. Crime introducing the story, drawn by Norman Maurer. *Public domain.*

Right: This Charles Biro–drawn cover of the comic book *Crime Does Not Pay* advertises "All True Crime Stories!" *Public domain.*

THE SHOOTING OF DULEY THE WRESTLING COP

One of the elements that was left out of the comic book version of the story is how it all began. It started in the summer of 1930, with Ray Sutherland's son Vaude, who was a twenty-year-old small-time moonshiner. The night before, Vaude had made a deal to sell a Mr. Stuman two gallons of moonshine the following day. Unbeknownst to Vaude, Stuman was recently out of jail after serving time on a charge of robbery with a dangerous weapon and had agreed to be an undercover agent, also known as a "stool pigeon," for Officer Oscar Duley.

Stuman, his wife and Officer Duley—in plain clothes, no uniform—made their way to the farm of Vaude's mother, Flora Irish. Flora had divorced Ray twenty years earlier because of his "brutal treatment." The farm was located on Wedling Road in Marcola, Oregon. Vaude lived on the property in a little shack with his twenty-year-old wife and eighteen-month-old child.

Duley must have assumed that this would be an easy affair: make the deal, arrest Vaude and be off at a normal time, because he did have plans that night. Officer Duley was known as Duley the Wrestling Cop, and he had an event scheduled that evening at the Lane County Fair. His wrestling skills would not come into play in this encounter.

When the Stumans and Duley drove up to Vaude's little shack, Vaude came out and instructed them to drive down the road a bit, turn around and meet him on the way back. Then he would have the liquor for them. Instead of doing that, Duley stepped out of the car onto the running board and told Vaude that he was under arrest.

Ray Sutherland, who had been hiding behind some ferns, possibly just in case of this kind of scenario, decided to shoot at the officer. Duley responded with two ineffective shots as Ray's bullets tore through his body and head. Duley died on the scene.

Ray then took off to the main house, the house of his ex-wife Flora. Once he saw her, he told her, "I got one of them! I'm going home and shoot it out with them." This is exactly what he did: he went home, armed himself and waited in a nice hiding spot for the authorities to show.

The Irish residence on Wendling road, many years later, in 1986. *Courtesy of the Lane County History Museum.*

From his ex-wife comes much of the biographical information about Ray. She was interviewed about the incident and about Ray himself. She said that for many years after their marriage, he worked infrequently but was a successful gambler. She also told them that one of his hands had an injury that left it shriveled and painful at times—although he was still able to use the hand for shooting. The story went that Ray always carried a gun and once, while he was unholstering the firearm, it went off and shot him through the hand. According to the *Oregonian*, Flora laughed after telling that story.

Ray's Shack

Later that night, acting on the tip from Flora, two deputies and a game warden showed up at Ray's shack. The two deputies were Joe Saunders and Lee Bown. Bown was the son of the county sheriff, Harry Bown. The game warden was Rodney Roach, who was also a special officer.

The officers brought bloodhounds to aid in their search for Ray, but the dogs were of little help in locating him. The comic book version of the story depicted Ray taking an onion bath to make sure that the dogs wouldn't go after his scent. The true reason that the dogs didn't smell Ray as he hid behind a partition is unknown.

From his hiding spot, Ray must have been watching the officers search his property, waiting for the perfect opportunity to make his move. Once the right moment came, with a .22 in one hand and .38 in the other, he took aim and shot at the officers. Only one of his shots missed their target. Ray sent two lethal bullets through Joe Saunders's heart, killing him. Lee Bown then turned to fire at Ray, but Ray was quicker, and he shot Bown in the elbow. This caused Bown to drop his gun and fall to the ground. With Bown neutralized, Ray took aim at Rodney Roach and shot him in the leg, dropping him to the floor as well. The only furniture in the room was a lone bed, so Roach and Bown made their way to hide behind it. Roach picked up Bown's gun along the way and waited for an opportunity to get a good shot. Ray was waiting for a good opportunity as well, and after Ray took a shot at their feet under the bed, Roach opened fire on him; bullets hit his abdomen and one of his hands. Ray retreated, leaving a trail of blood behind him as he ran from the shack.

Lee Bown and Rodney Roach were in bad shape but were able to make their way to their automobile. It was said that because of their injuries, Bown had to work the pedals while Roach handled the shifting and steering. With teamwork, they were able to drive the car to a rendezvous point where other officers and Vaude Sutherland were waiting. Once they arrived there, they were put in another vehicle and rushed to the hospital.

Now, the rest of the posse had the unfortunate task of going back to the shack and retrieving the body of Joe Saunders, not knowing if Ray Sutherland was still there or not, possibly waiting to kill more officers.

Fearing this, they had a plan: the first person to enter the shack would be the one person they assumed Ray wouldn't shoot, Vaude. They tied a rope around Vaude and sent him into the cabin alone. Once it was clear that Ray was gone, they entered and removed the body.

When Ray left the cabin, he ran through the thick wilderness to the Mohawk River and followed it back to his ex-wife's house so she could treat his wounds. From there, he disappeared.

RAY THE FUGITIVE

When Sheriff Harry Bown heard of what went down, he was quite motivated to catch Ray; not only had Ray now killed two of his deputies, but he had also wounded a game warden and Deputy Lee Bown, the sheriff's son. This was Harry's second run as sheriff. His first was from 1906 to 1913. In those years, he was trying to catch the McKenzie River Bandits. Before he could, he was replaced by James C. Parker, who got the job done.

After James Parker, three more people served as sheriff of Lane County before Harry got his chance again in 1929. Harry Bown had a good reputation; according to the history section of the official Lane County website, Bown was known as a "pure law man" and a "natural born manhunter."

Harry conducted a monthlong manhunt for Ray, with little success. During their search, the authorities brought machine guns on a couple of occasions. There was even a $500 dollar dead or alive reward offered.

The newspapers didn't let up on the story, either; they ran stories about people who thought they saw Ray and frequently asked the sheriff's department: "Caught Sutherland yet?" or "Where do you think Sutherland is hiding?"

The public had a few theories about where Sutherland might be. It was said that he had wielded a strange fear over the heads of some residents. Some people even referred to him as a sinister figure. It was known that he always carried a gun and he was a deadly shot. So, it is possible that he was holding up with someone who was too fearful to turn him in. There were

Harry Bown in the sheriff's office at the Lane County Courthouse. *Courtesy of the Lane County History Museum.*

rumors that he was helped out of the area by automobile or maybe even by train. Others believed that he was dead—not dead from his wounds but possibly by his own hand.

If anyone did know where he was, he must have had a hold on them, because no one tried to claim that $500 dead or alive reward or the eventual $2,000 reward that was offered for his capture. With a price tag that high on your head, you better trust the people around you.

One of the first sightings of Sutherland was by Dell S. Goe, a barber who claimed a man matching Sutherland's description came into his shop for a shave. During the shave, the man tried to explain why he was unkempt by stating that he just returned from a hunting trip.

Vaude Sutherland had his trial two months later, while his father was still missing. Vaude was not charged with any violence. He was sentenced to two months and a $250 fine for possession of liquor. They couldn't get him on distribution, since he never handed the liquor over to the deputy or the two "undercover agents." Vaude was taken to Portland, where he would work off his sentence and the fine at the Kelly Butte rock pile.

Ray's Last Shootout

A month later, Ray Sutherland was finally found in the woods a mile east of Westfir and a half mile from the Willamette Highway. Westfir was a small mill town about fifteen miles south of Marcola, where this story began. Westfir had a population of 500 people at the time. As of the 2020 census, the town was down to a population of 315.

Ray Sutherland had been spending his time between a cabin and a lean-to in the woods that he would sleep in so he wouldn't get caught off guard. His lean-to was impressive; it was made from two fallen trees with a shake roof. The fallen trees were lying across each other, forming a *V*. The *V* of Sutherland's hideout worked to his advantage. If anyone approached his hideout by way of the road, he had an open area to shoot from. The only problem is that the posse of sheriffs and deputies that had been searching for him for the last ten days didn't come from that direction.

The posse was sent by Sheriff Harry Bown. John Carlile was the leader of the group. His son Lester Carlile was also a member. Walter Edmiston, a deputy sheriff, was another member; he carried a .25-20 Winchester rifle with him. The last three men were Ward "Taxi" Lonsberry, Fred Petzold and Clayton Inman. Inman carried a .30-30 rifle.

The posse found the cabin first, and from there, they were able to track Sutherland to the lean-to. Lester Carlile and Fred Petzold were the first to approach the lean-to. Lester was the one who spotted Ray. Ray spotted them, too, when he rolled over in his bed.

Some reports say that Ray immediately fired a shot at the posse. John Carlile stated the same at the trial. Clayton Inman, at trial, said that one of the deputies yelled for him to come out and surrender before Ray took a shot. Walter Edmiston testified that this was true and said, "I hollered at him to come out from behind the log, and just then he fired at us, he fired two shots as we were advancing." Edmiston also stated that he believed Ray heard them approaching and was ready for a fight.

Once Ray took that first shot, it was on. Lester Carlile and Petzold opened fire and told the other men to stay back. The four moved into a small depression in the ground. Ray shot in the direction of the four, but the small depression was just deep enough that the shots went over their heads.

The four men then scattered and surrounded Ray's hiding spot and started firing back. Ray continued shooting at them from under the log. Lonsberry had a bullet go just over his head. The gunfire was coming quickly and from all angles, so Ray couldn't take time to get a good shot. He would just put up his left arm from out of the logs and shoot at random. Petzold used this as an opportunity and shot through the opening that Ray's hand came out from. This shot hit Ray. With Ray hit, John Carlile then ran around to the opening of the *V* and started exchanging shots with Ray. The other men continued shooting as well, while groans from Ray were heard from time to time. Edmiston emptied both of his guns in the battle, and it was said that most of the other men did as well.

Ray's last attempt was a shot at John Carlile when Carlile was about ten feet away from him. His shot missed. John Carlile and Lester Carlile then fired at Ray. Both of their shots hit him in the head, blasting pieces away and killing him. His bullet-ridden body slumped over.

Sheriff Harry Bown was alerted to the incident and headed down there to investigate. With him were his son Lee and Rodney Roach, who were both still healing from being shot by Ray.

Vaude Sutherland, who was working at the rock pile at Kelly Butte, was informed of his father's death via telephone.

Later, a reporter came to Kelly Butte and interviewed Vaude in the kitchen there. Vaude had a lot to say about his father. He told the reporter how they weren't that close: "I was never with him long but he always treated me alright. He worked in the woods all his life." Vaude said that Ray was not a moonshiner: "That was all bunk about his running a can. He didn't know how to make whiskey. I know, because he asked me several times how to do it. Yes, I know how; I ran a 'can' a couple years ago." Vaude then went on to say, "So far as I know Dad hadn't been handling liquor until a short time ago and then he sold only a few bottles. He had always been quite a gambler but I don't think he sold whiskey before."

Vaude was asked what he would do after his sentence was through. Vaude said, "Then I'm going to leave the state and go to work.…I'm through with liquor, of course, I may drink it, but I won't make it or sell it. That [has] been a lesson to me."

Vaude might have gone straight after this; there are no other mentions of him and moonshining in the papers. He didn't leave the state like he said he would, though. He went on to work in the logging business in Oregon.

In April 1939, Vaude was struck by a small tree that snapped back into place after being pulled to one side by a trip line. He was taken to a hospital, but he died, leaving his wife and two daughters behind.

PART V

FINAL BUSTS AND THE END OF PROHIBITION

CHAPTER 15

TUSKO'S TEN-GALLON TODDY

Tusko was a giant elephant. Various weights and measurements have been reported over the years. He weighed anywhere from twelve to eighteen thousand pounds at the time of our story, and he was over twelve feet tall—some articles say twelve foot two, while some say twelve foot seven. While his height and weight are inconsistent between stories, one form of measurement involving Tusko is consistent in each article. That is the amount of moonshine Tusko's owner gave him that night in December 1931 when he wasn't feeling too well. It was ten gallons.

There was a potential danger with this home remedy. Tusko had a rumored history with moonshine. In 1922, he escaped from the Al G. Barnes Circus while it was in Sedro-Woolley, Washington. He allegedly knocked around a couple of cars, knocked a garage off its foundation and destroyed most of a barn, as well as various chicken coops. None of the articles printed in 1922 mention moonshine, but a later article retells the incident and describes a scene in which Tusko found himself a moonshine still running at "full blast" and drank himself fifty gallons' worth.

Tusko's 1931 moonshine incident in Oregon was less dramatic. He was older and near the end of his career. Tusko first arrived in North America in 1898 and changed hands a few times over the years. For many years, he was an attraction for the Al G. Barnes Circus, where at times he was billed as "the Largest Elephant in Captivity" and as "the Meanest Elephant."

Later, Al Painter became the owner of Tusko. Painter exhibited him at Lotus Isle Amusement Park, a short-lived amusement park in Portland,

Al Painter billed the elephant as "Tusko the Magnificent" during its time at Lotus Isle in Portland, Oregon. *Courtesy of Stephen Kenny.*

Oregon, that lasted only from 1930 to 1932. During his time at Lotus Isle, Tusko was kept behind the Peacock Ballroom, a beautiful building modeled after the Hagia Sophia in Constantinople with a one-hundred-foot gold dome. His conditions behind the Peacock were a far cry from glamorous, and complaints were made to the Oregon Humane Society about the conditions.

An incident happened while Tusko was at Lotus Isle. A low-flying plane spooked him, which made him break free from his chains. Before he could be stopped, he wrecked several pavilions.

Tusko's next stop was the Oregon State Fair. When the fair ended, the poor elephant was abandoned. Eventually, he would be purchased by Jack O'Grady and Bernard Gray and moved back up to Portland. O'Grady and Gray's plan was to walk him to New York in the spring to sell him. They would have to walk him because he had grown too large for a railcar. Their hope was to exhibit him along the way, charging a dime to see him.

In Portland, he was kept in a shed on East Main Street. There were plans to move him, but he was too despondent. Articles referred to him as being temporarily insane. Tusko was merely in musth.

Mayor of Portland George Baker spoke to the press about the elephant and was quoted as saying,

> *It looks like we are host whether we want to be or not. He is not the sort of animal we can drop on the highway or dump into somebody's yard, so we are going to do the only thing we can do, he is properly secured and every effort will be made to keep the place sanitary.*

The shed Tusko inhabited was in poor condition and barely kept the cold air out. Tusko got sick, and there seemed to be nothing to be done about it. But then Jack O'Grady, one of his owners, procured ten gallons of moonshine for Tusko. It did appear that Tusko had a history with liquor, because as soon as the moonshine was brought into the shed, Tusko got excited and started slapping his trunk on the ground. Once the mixture of ten gallons of "moon," as his handler called it, and five gallons of water was in reach, Tusko took a big gulp, emptying half the tub of booze. Quite quickly, the world's largest shot of whiskey was inside the giant elephant, and he was happy about it.

Tusko's joy was evident while he played with a bale of hay for five minutes, flipping it over and over. Then he grabbed a large piece of wood and played with it like a toothpick. In his drunken state, Tusko accidentally got it lodged in his mouth, and it took three men to pull it out. After a while, Tusko got tired, so he lay down on his bed made of hay and went to sleep.

The next day, Tusko had a hangover big enough to make the front page of the *Sunday Oregonian*. The paper reported that he had bloodshot eyes and hanging skin. It was also stated that nothing would make him feel better. Tusko was offered polished apples that were donated by the Ladd Grocery Store, but he refused them. He just wanted more moonshine. He sniffed at the empty tub that once held the giant cocktail; finding it empty, he tossed it aside.

A few days later, it was reported that Tusko had hiccups from his hangover. Supposedly, his handlers cured this ailment of his via the hair-of-the-dog route. Tusko was given a small hot toddy—well, small for him. This time, it was made from only one gallon of moonshine, a quart of lemon juice, a pound of sugar and hot water. After this, Tusko was reported to be a new elephant.

Another development that probably helped his health more than the "moon" was the installation of a wood-burning stove in his shack to keep him warm. Later in the month, he would destroy much of that shack during an escape attempt on Christmas Day.

This incident drew a large crowd of onlookers, as well as a squad of police officers and National Guardsmen who were armed with submachine guns and high-powered rifles. They were prepared to kill Tusko. Luckily for the elephant, Mayor Baker told them to hold off unless he broke completely free, which he never did. One local man named Phil Holliman devised a trap for Tusko: he hid a loop of cable under some hay and then placed carrots nearby. When Tusko put his leg in the spot, the cable was pulled taut and secured. Then it was just a matter of securing the other leg.

Tusko had worn out his welcome in Oregon, and at the time of his death from a blood clot in June 1933, he was a resident of the Seattle Zoo. Years later, in 1954, Tusko returned to Oregon for good when his bones were donated to the University of Oregon.

CHAPTER 16

MURDER IN FRONT OF THE MAJESTIC IN CORVALLIS

The last few years had not been great for Elijah "E.B." Mills. In 1927, his wife divorced him and moved to Ventura, California, with their daughter. In 1928, he got busted with sixteen pints of moonshine in the basement of his restaurant called the Corvallis Grill. It was a popular local restaurant, and it was once written that Mr. Mills was one of the best cooks in the city. An ad he ran for his restaurant read, "To dine here is truly a delight," and "Stop here before or after the theater."

Those were bad years, but the big trouble came in November 1930 after a series of bad choices finally caught up with Mills. One of the mistakes he made was upsetting another moonshiner named William "Bill" Henderson. Part of the issue stemmed from a card game that the two were in; Henderson lost money and later found out that Mills was cheating by using marked cards. The other thing about Mills that rubbed Henderson the wrong way was that he was a "hijacker." Mills liked to rob other moonshine outfits of their product when they were passing near Corvallis.

The feud went back at least as far as May of that year, according to F.A. Thrasher, a local grocer who told a story about running into Mills in the Club Cigar Shop and Pool Hall. According to him, Mills was drinking and told him that a certain individual had a warrant out for him, but Mills said that if approached, he would kill him on the spot. Then that individual came into the cigar shop. Thrasher told the man about Mills's threat. That man then approached Mills, and the two stared at each other. Thrasher said that not a word was spoken between the two before the other man turned around and left the store. With that man gone, Mills continued to tell Thrasher about his troubles, and according to him, Mills said there was another man who would die with his boots on. He told Thrasher that man was Bill Henderson.

Bill Henderson was a longtime moonshiner; his arrest records go back to at least 1925, when he was busted on the road with moonshine. Henderson and a man named "Buck" Hardwick were involved in a police chase while transporting 'shine in an Oldsmobile touring car. During the chase, Officer Browne fired at the vehicle. Hardwick tried to save them a bit of jail time by throwing out the jugs filled with moonshine before they pulled over, but enough was able to be saved from the broken bottles for a conviction.

Bill Henderson was angry enough with E.B. Mills that he tipped off the Benton County Sheriff's Office about Mills's plan to "hijack" another moonshiner on the road and steal the liquor that he was hauling. He gave this tip to a local officer who worked nights around the area that they frequented. This officer's name was Fred Thompson. Tipping off the cops wouldn't be the worst thing that Henderson would do to Mills before the end of 1930.

The Sheriff's Department took the tip seriously and set up a few officers on the highway to watch out for the car that was moving the liquor, as well as for the potential hijacker.

Deputy Sheriff Carl Schloeman set himself up in Lewisburg, while a couple of traffic officers, Earl Humphrey and Mace Peutherer, went and searched the highways.

They were about eleven miles outside of Corvallis when they saw two cars on the side of the highway near Joe Brown Road. Could this be the load of 'shine they were looking for? Was the second car full of moonshine as well, or was it the hijacker? The second car would remain a mystery for the moment, because it was gone by the time they parked their police car alongside the first. The first car was a Portland taxi, and as soon as Peutherer stepped out of his vehicle, he saw the back of the taxi was full of kegs of alcohol.

The two didn't bother going after the other vehicle. They arrested the people in the car and took the car with them to where Carl Schloeman was waiting.

Once the car and the people were with Deputy Schloeman, Humphrey and Peutherer were back on the road looking for the second vehicle and/or the potential hijacker. They brought along two of the captured moonshine runners, who admitted that they were to deliver the moonshine to Eddyville. Eventually, they admitted to the officers that the other vehicle was also a Portland taxi and it, too, was filled with booze.

The group headed toward Eddyville, and after a short while, a large roadster drove past them—not the Portland taxi they were looking for. They followed the roadster past Eddyville but eventually turned back toward the town. Soon after, the roadster showed back up. This time, when they followed it, it took off. They quickened their speed, and a car chase ensued.

The *Corvallis Gazette-Times* reported that "the two cars roared over the Corvallis-Newport highway. Many places going over 60 miles an hour." The car chase spanned fifteen miles before ending when the roadster pulled over to the side of the road near the town of Burnt Woods. Then two of the occupants jumped out and ran into the woods, leaving the driver behind. The driver, Jess Crawford was arrested, and the officers found a concealed weapon on him.

While the chase was going on, the other Portland taxi showed up where Deputy Schloeman and the first Portland taxi they confiscated were sitting. The driver of this second taxi got out but quickly returned to his car after one of the arrested moonshiners yelled out, "The bulls are on the job." *Bulls* was a slang term for the police, more common in the early part of the twentieth century; the term alluded to how aggressive some officers could be. The driver took the hint, jumped back in his car and took off, not to be seen again. Deputy Schloeman could not chase after him, since he had the other car in tow.

E.B. Mills was not busted that night, but he also didn't get the booze he was after.

According to later reports, E.B. Mills left town not too long after. This was after Bill Henderson threatened him, telling him that he "better get out and stay out!" Mills left for a few days to Marshfield, a town on the coast of Oregon that is now known as Coos Bay.

E.B. Mills didn't stay gone for long. When he came back to town, he got together with a group and went to a local restaurant, where they discussed the Henderson issue. At his table was a woman named Miss Emma, a man named Warren Brown and Quint Garrett, a moonshiner in his own right.

Quint was also on the outs with Henderson over a card game that Henderson claimed was crooked. Quint Garret, besides working with Mills, also worked with his brother Wyman Garrett.

Wyman was busted a few months back. At the time, he was with a man allegedly named Bus Hiller. They were spotted along the river with moonshine that they were draining into smaller bottles for distribution. Wyman and Hiller saw the officers coming and started throwing the bottles in the river to get rid of the evidence. Then, before the officers got to them, Hillman ran off and escaped into the woods.

Wyman was not able to get rid of all the bottles in time. The officers found a single bottle half-filled with moonshine, enough for a charge, but while the officers were talking to Wyman, he was able to grab the bottle out of the officer's hand and throw it in the river, as well.

The officers might have been more upset, but they eventually found a bottle that got caught in the brush along the side of the river. With evidence secured, Wyman was arrested. He served a thirty-day sentence in the county jail for that incident.

During their meal, E.B. Mills told his group that neither Henderson nor anyone else would run him out of town. He also allegedly told them that in regards to Henderson, he had someone who would "take him out." If that person existed, he was slow to get Henderson, because Henderson and Mills and would end their conflict with each other less than a week later, on November 29, in front of the Majestic Theater on Second Street in Corvallis, Oregon.

A young Wyman Garrett (*front row, third from left*) and a young Quint Garrett (*third row, second from left*). *Courtesy of Benton County Historical Society.*

The Pastime Pool Hall store, where you could get your Magnus Root Beer or your cigars. The sign above the entryway to the pool hall says, "If Not 21, Stay Out." *Courtesy of Benton County Historical Society.*

On that night, trouble began in an establishment called the Pastime Pool Hall, located downstairs in the Hotel Julian. Across the hall from the Pastime was the barbershop where Henderson used to be a barber before moonshining became his trade. He must have still had keys to the barbershop, because it was reported later by George Ernest, when he was on the witness stand, that he saw Henderson in there shaving that night. It's possible that Henderson wanted to look his best for either outcome that might came from that night. He was either going to leave a good-looking corpse or look his best for the mug shot.

All the players were down in the Pastime at some point: Bill Henderson, E.B. Mills, Quint Garrett and another one of Mills's associates, Joe Harkins.

Joe Harkins was a career criminal. His first publicized incident involved him getting caught by Sheriff J.E. Lillard in a car carrying stolen items from a wrecked vehicle. Harkins and a buddy had been driving around and saw a wrecked car. Harkins stole the horn and an inner tube from the vehicle. For that bust, he had to pay a twenty-five-dollar fine. Less than a month after that, Harkins was busted again by J.E. Lillard, this time for reckless driving. The following year, at the age of nineteen, he was busted for selling moonshine on the streets of Corvallis. He was caught making a deal in an alley by Chief Robinson. His latest bust was also a liquor possession charge; this time, he was released on $500 bail. At this point, he hadn't been caught making moonshine himself, so he was probably a dealer.

The Pastime might have been a straight establishment; there are no records of it selling liquor. It also seemed like most of the mens' drinking was done in the bathroom. Quint Garrett was involved in an incident earlier that week with Henderson in that bathroom—that is, if the testimony he gave in court later was truthful. According to Quint, Henderson came into the bathroom and said, "I want three hundred dollars or you are dead (blankety-blank)." (The "blankety-blank" is courtesy of the *Corvallis Gazette-Times*; the paper printed the transcription and knew that its readership would be up in arms if it printed the real words he said.) Quint replied to Henderson, "You can't have three hundred dollars, I haven't got it." Quint then said, "Bill, you wasn't beat crooked in that game." Quint did admit that he did play crooked cards against Henderson on a different night, so he asked Henderson how much he lost on that night. Henderson claimed it was $108. Quint paid him, which might just have saved him that night. Henderson made no direct threats but told Quint that he was going to make Mills pay, as well.

On the night of November 29, Quint, Joe Harkins and a couple of other guys were in the bathroom of the Pastime having a drink. Henderson had been seen that night around the Pastime but wasn't in there with them. E.B. Mills eventually came in, joined the conversation and had himself a drink that was offered to him. Then Henderson came in, fired up, and according to Quint's testimony, Henderson put his hand on Mills's neck and said, "Hello, you old hijacker." Mills's response was calm; he either said, "Hello, Bill," or "How are you, Bill?" Quint claimed that was all that was said and that Henderson was offered a drink, but he refused it.

After a while, E.B. Mills told the men that "Emma has my car outside so I guess I'll go up." It was early in the evening, only eight o'clock. Mills then climbed the stairs, not noticing that Henderson was following him.

Mills's car was parked in front of the Majestic Theater, and a lady friend of his known only as Miss Emma was sitting inside. As Mills walked to his car, Bill pulled out his gun, a .32 automatic, from a pocket in his overcoat.

The fact that there were many people on the street that night did not deter Henderson. Mills made it to his car and was just about to get in when Henderson, at about six feet from Mills, pointed the gun and pulled the trigger. Later, an autopsy would reveal that the single bullet entered

In this photo, you can see that the Majestic was right next door to the Hotel Julian; in the basement of that hotel was the Pastime Pool Hall. *Courtesy of Benton County Historical Society.*

Mills's left shoulder and traveled through to just above his heart, severing the main artery.

The next thing Henderson needed to do was get rid of the murder weapon. This was important to do if he wanted to get away with the killing, but with all the witnesses, his chances of getting away with it were slim. Not only were there witnesses, but there was also a cop nearby. Fred Thompson, the night officer Henderson had blabbed about Mills to, was in the Club Cigar Store when he was alerted that someone had been shot.

Before Henderson could run and get rid of the gun, Officer Fred Thompson was on the scene and told him to halt. Henderson did not halt but yelled back to the officer that he would be back. The *Corvallis Gazette-Times* quoted him as saying to the officer, "You stay where you are, I'll be right back." With that, he was off; he ran past the Hotel, Julian took a right and ran to the Willamette River, which was less than eight hundred feet from the Majestic. Once he was at the river, he tossed the revolver into the water and then made his way back to the scene of the crime to turn himself in.

Henderson would admit to the shooting but gave no reason other than to say, according to Thompson's testimony, that "he felt as though he had done his duty." Thompson also claimed Henderson had said, "I wonder why in *hell* Mills didn't stay out of town." Of course, when the quote ran in the *Corvallis Gazette-Times, hell* was written "H—l."

It wasn't long after Mills's death that the rumors started. According to the *Evening Herald*, there were rumors that he was "put on the spot" for his alleged hijackings of other bootleggers' liquor. Henderson refused to deny or confirm this information. He was keeping his mouth shut until the trial—which gave him plenty of time to craft his version of the story.

Henderson's version was that it was a self-defense situation. When he was asked at trial why he was carrying a gun that night, he explained:

> *I started packing a gun in self-defense after I had received a telephone call from Joe Harkins asking me to meet him someplace but not telling me what business was the purpose of the proposed meeting, a meeting which I refused to make, and then being told by Harkins that I would meet him at some other time and would be sorry that I did not meet him at this time.*

The rest of Henderson's version of the events of that night goes like this. He went outside to find his car and find out if his wife had finished shopping. When he was in front of the Majestic, he spotted Mills standing by his car with a peculiar expression on his face. The face Mills was making was so out of the ordinary that Henderson took a couple of steps toward him. But Mills took a couple of steps backward in response and reached toward his hip pocket. Henderson stated that he thought Mills was going to pull out a gun. Fearing that Mills would shoot him without hesitation, Henderson pulled out his gun and shot Mills first.

No gun was found on Mills. But during the trial, some witnesses gave testimony that Quint Garrett was seen near the car and the body, implying that Garrett might have taken the gun in question.

Another aspect that was brought up is that Mill's body was found a couple of steps away from the door of his car. This could be for two reasons. Mills might have been trying to get behind his car to shield himself, or he might have been going for the sawed-off shotgun that was later found in his trunk.

During the trial, many witnesses were called on both sides. The defense tried to prove that E.B. Mills was the aggressor and that Mills, Joe Harkins and Quint Garrett were a rough group of characters. Henderson claimed self-defense throughout the trial, and Officer Fred Thompson testified that he had warned Henderson he should be careful.

The jury ended up not going for first-degree murder. Henderson was sentenced to ten years in prison on a manslaughter charge. During the closing of the trial, Judge Skipworth told Henderson that he was "extremely fortunate," because there was "ample" evidence for a first-degree charge.

Henderson left the courtroom in a good mood. He told someone that he was "lucky." Friends of Henderson attended the trial and gave their goodbyes and said they were glad he had only received a ten-year sentence.

The trial ended in January 1931. Prohibition would continue for another couple years, and during that time, both Quint Garrett and Joe Harkins would make the papers again for moonshining-related crimes.

Quint Garrett got in trouble a few weeks after the trial with his other brother, Stacey, and a man named James Marr. The trouble started when Dale Hunt, a local man, turned Wyman Garrett in for moonshining. In response, Quint, Stay and James went over to Dale Hunt's house to teach him a lesson. The beating was brutal and included repeated blows to Hunt's face. He was left bloody and in need of medical attention. Once the three men left, Hunt made his way to Dr. Fortmiller's house. Hunt was bleeding so profusely that there was blood left on his door and all over the front porch.

Joe Harkin had seemingly given up on the "hijacking" game and started up his own moonshine still. In September 1932, his little operation was surrounded by Sheriff Newton, Deputy Carl Schloeman, Deputy Earl Humphrey, Deputy Bill Mynatt and, of course, J.E. Lillard, who had arrested Harkins many times throughout his life.

During the raid, the officers surrounded all the buildings of Harkins's operation near Oak Creek, three miles outside of Corvallis. The first officers that Joe spotted were Newton and Humphry. After seeing them, he took off but ended up running into the area that Deputy Mynatt and J.E. Lillard were in. Mynatt yelled for him to stop running. Harkin didn't heed the call, so Mynatt chased after him for one hundred yards or so before firing at his legs with a shotgun. Two buckshots entered his legs without doing much damage, but they did knock him down so that the arrest could be made.

At his operation, the authorities captured a fifty-gallon still, one hundred gallons of mash and about four gallons of finished moonshine. Harkins was given one year in prison. By the time he would get out, Prohibition would nearly be over.

CHAPTER 17

THE END OF AN ERA

Moonshining on a grand scale ended around the same time the great experiment called Prohibition ended. From 1931 to 1933, the number of people making alcohol seemed to be going down. Some of this is likely from the effects of the Great Depression. There were also some laws that changed regarding enforcement in Oregon in those years, as well as the eventual return of beer. Here is the history of some of the more interesting busts in those last few years before Prohibition ended on December 5, 1933.

A BAD DEAL IN MEDFORD

In February 1932, Joseph Hand, a forty-two-year-old logger, and his much younger, twenty-three-year-old partner, Carl Thomas, got busted after making a deal in which they traded moonshine for an automobile from a couple of undercover Prohibition agents.

The story goes that in December 1931, Hand and Thomas made it known around Medford that they were looking to get a used automobile and that they were willing to trade moonshine for said vehicle. Harry Holland, a Prohibition agent, and Art Johnson, a state police officer, got wind of this and contacted the two. Hand and Thomas had to admit that they did not have much of a supply at the time but stated that they would by the first of February.

The deal was made that they would trade thirty gallons of homemade whiskey for a coupe or sixty gallons for a sedan. The value of a sedan versus the value of a coupe has changed over the years. Now, when it comes to vintage or antique cars, a coupe can be worth thousands more.

The authorities added a few interesting requirements to the deal. The moonshine had to be uncolored, free from charcoal and in wax-sealed barrels. They also insisted on being able to test the moonshine to see that it was over one hundred proof. All that seems fair, but the thing that should have tipped off Hand and Thomas was that the authorities insisted they be able to see the still. Their given reason was to make sure it was sanitary.

February first came, and instead of receiving the moonshine, the officers received a letter stating that the cold weather had slowed Hand and Thomas down, but they would be ready to make the deal on the fifth.

On the fifth, the Prohibition agent and the police officer showed up at the cabin of the two men. First, they inspected the twenty-five-gallon-capacity still, and then they tested the liquor. Once that was done, they made the deal with the moonshiners. For thirty gallons of the 'shine, they would be given a 1930 Ford Coupe.

The moonshine was valued at eight dollars a gallon, a good buy for the Ford Coupe—the car was $500 new. Officer Holland stated that the both the value of the automobile and the 'shine had less value because of the Depression.

The Depression was, of course, all over the newspapers at that time and did seem to affect the illegal booze trade. The *Medford Mail Tribune* reported that attendance at the local dances was down, for a reason. Sheriff Ralph Jennings was quoted as saying, "People are too hard up to buy moonshine." Another quote from that article comes from a moonshiner who got busted; he said, "You people might as well have it; you can't sell the stuff anymore."

After the trade, the liquor was loaded into a couple of sedans for transportation. Once that was taken care of, all that was left was for the agents to flash their badges and for the two to be hauled off to jail.

A BIG BLAST IN SALEM

An explosion ended the moonshine career of John Coryell in April 1932. Coryell rented a house on North Front Street in Salem from Mrs. Cora Hendry only a week before the incident. According to her testimony, Coryell did not tell her that he was going to use her property as a place to make illegal moonshine liquor. The still he installed was a wash-boiler type with copper cooling coils. He was using cracked corn to create his mash. He was also using a gas generator, which is what exploded and set the house on fire.

Neighbors told a reporter for the *Statesman Journal* that they heard the blast around four thirty in the afternoon, and when they looked toward the house, they saw a man running away. There was still a mass of flames inside when the fire trucks rolled up. They were able to put the fire out in short order, but the inner walls of three of the rooms were destroyed.

When Mrs. Hendry, the owner, arrived, the fire was already out. She entered the home to inspect the damage, and as soon as she saw the moonshine still, she called the police. The police found John Coryell nearby and arrested him. John pleaded guilty to a charge of unlawful possession of intoxicating liquor and had to spend fifty days in the city jail.

WE ADVOCATE THE REPEAL OF THE EIGHTEENTH AMENDMENT

By the summer of 1932, the idea of a repeal of the Eighteenth Amendment was picking up steam. The Democratic Party was running on many tenets, but for many Americans, the most important part of its 1932 platform was its views on Prohibition. Here is a section from the platform:

> *We advocate the repeal of the Eighteenth Amendment. To effect such repeal we demand that the Congress immediately propose a Constitutional Amendment to truly represent the conventions in the states called to act solely on that proposal; we urge the enactment of such measures by the several states as will actually promote temperance, effectively prevent the return of the saloon, and bring the liquor traffic into the open under complete supervision and control by the states.*

Another section of the same platform:

> *Pending repeal, we favor immediate modification of the Volstead Act; to legalize the manufacture and sale of beer and other beverages of such alcoholic content as is permissible under the Constitution and to provide therefrom a proper and needed revenue.*

MOONSHINERS OF KLAMATH FALLS

In September 1932, Raymond Dawson and Cliff Johnson's nice little moonshine operation in Klamath Falls was being searched for by authorities. Someone had talked and let the police know that there was some moonshining going on in the general area around Williams Street.

With this tip, Sergeant Carl Cook and Officer Hayes started taking turns going to the area to look for the illegal distillery. Their main plan was to try to sniff around to get the scent of mash. If they could get a hint of the smell, they thought they just might be able to follow it to the still.

Eventually, their noses did catch a whiff of the corn mash, and they were able to follow it to an empty-looking house. Using the scent of the corn mash as probable cause, they entered the dwelling. Inside, they found a forty-five-gallon-capacity still and seven barrels of mash that had electric glow lights on them keeping them at a good temperature. This wasn't an amateur operation. During their search, they also found cracked corn, barley, sugar, kegs and gallon jugs. What they failed to find was the moonshiners themselves.

Sergeant Cook and Officer Hayes decided that the best course of action was to wait for the moonshiners to return to bust them. They stayed there all night. At six thirty in the morning, while Sergeant Cook was struggling to make coffee using one of the glow lights for heat, they heard a key being put in the door lock. In response, Hayes pulled out his gun and yelled out, "Come right in boys." After that, they could hear the footsteps of the two men running off.

Haynes was quick to run after the two men as they sped through the grass, and he only had to fire his gun twice in the air before the two stopped running. When the sergeant caught up with Hayes, he could see that Hayes had the situation handled. Both criminals stood motionless as they stared down the barrel of Hayes's gun.

During their trial, Dawson and Johnson claimed that the still was not theirs and they were just coming by to buy a gallon of moonshine. One problem with this defense was that Dawson had a prior liquor offense. When he was on the stand being cross-examined, he admitted to getting in trouble eight years previously for liquor charges in the same county. For that bust, he told the court that he served a sentence of sixteen months in jail. A search for that story in the old newspapers from around that time reveals a story that Dawson's wife was not too happy with his illegal activities. She filed for divorce while he was in prison because of his moonshining. She complained that she had repeatedly pleaded for him to stop selling moonshine and that he would not stop.

The trial did not end in Dawson and Johnson's favor. Both men were found guilty of possession of a still.

THE AMERICAN LEGION IN PORTLAND

In September 1932, there was a big push to make Portland dry during the large American Legion National Convention that was happening from the twelfth to the fifteenth.

Maurice Smith, who was the Prohibition administrator for the Pacific Northwest, came down from his home in Seattle for the occasion. During this weekend, he was quoted as saying, "We are doing all that we can to stop the sale of liquor and other violations wherever they are found."

For moonshiners and bootleggers, they saw the convention as an opportunity to move a lot of product. One bootlegger named Ross Turney from California was caught heading through Oregon toward Portland with a trailer covered with American Legion banners. Inside was twenty-four gallons of bottled moonshine and several cases of gin. Captain Leo Bown of the state police said that he was trying to "camouflage, to cover up rum-running during the heavy auto travel to the national convention at Portland."

There were nightly raids during the convention. On the first night, the Prohibition officers raided a half dozen places with only one bust. It was a three-story former Lodge building that was once home to the Knights of Columbus. There, the officers found and confiscated fifty-one pints of moonshine. The only arrest was of the bartender.

The next night, officers raided the headquarters of the visiting members of the American Legion. One raid was of the Sixth Artillery Station. There they found 14 cases of beer and around 10 gallons of whiskey. The biggest haul of the night was the headquarters of the Eighteenth Engineers. There they found and seized 434 pints of moonshine, 86 gallons of alcohol of an unknown type, 60 quarts of gin and 21 quarts of wine. Lon V. Hamilton, who was allegedly in charge of the place, was arrested.

Arresting and raiding the headquarters of the American Legion must not have gone over well with the public, because after these raids, Maurice Smith gave an interview explaining his stance and took full responsibility. The papers had alleged that he had backup sent from D.C. to help with the raids. Smith was quick to say, "I take all the responsibility for the raids

In this photo, you can see how large a gathering there was for the American Legion National Convention. *Author's collection.*

of Prohibition operatives in Portland during the past few days. This is my problem. I am sworn to enforce the Prohibition law and I am trying to enforce it without favoritism or fear of consequences."

Some Legionnaires got themselves in trouble drinking. Three members got into a one-vehicle wreck with a telephone pole while driving at high speeds. Floyd Michaels, who was a local from Baker County, Oregon, died in the wreck. Gus Schlegger, who had traveled from Detroit, Michigan, for the event, had internal injuries. Attendants at the hospital said that he was in critical condition. Gardner Bushnell, a Portland local, had large cuts on his face from the accident. A partly filled bottle of moonshine was found in the wreckage.

ON THE BALLOT

Another strike against Prohibition as it affected Oregonians was Measure 7, which was on the November ballot of 1932. It passed with 59 percent of the vote in favor. The measure reads as follows:

Initiative Bill—Proposed by Initiative Petition—Vote YES or NO BILL
TO REPEAL STATE PROHIBITION LAW OF OREGON—
Purpose: To repeal the general prohibition law of the state of Oregon,

which prohibits the manufacture, sale, giving away, barter, delivery, receipt, possession, importation or transportation of intoxicating liquor within this state, and provides for the enforcement of such prohibition; and thus to do away with prohibition and its enforcement in and by the state of Oregon.

This did not end Prohibition in Oregon per se, as making alcohol for consumption was still illegal at the federal level, but an important part of the measure is that it took away some of the state's ability to enforce the federal Prohibition laws, leaving enforcement to the federal level, where there weren't enough agents to handle it. Without as much risk and not as much 'shine being lost to local authorities, the cost of moonshine dropped down to around one dollar per gallon in some areas.

This didn't end all alcohol laws in Oregon, as it was still illegal to drink and drive, of course, and still unlawful to operate an unlicensed still. But with the cost of the finished product going down, there were fewer and fewer people bothering to run a still.

End of 1932

There were not many more busts in the rest of 1932, just a few minor busts by local authorities of small-timers with unlicensed stills. At the end of December, as the local authorities lessened their efforts to bust moonshiners, Oregon saw an uptick of moonshiners being busted by Prohibition agents.

One of these busts involved a large still in Wallowa County on the property of A.G. Schnore. When caught, Schnore claimed that two other men operated the still and he just owned the property. One of those men was Marvin Horner. One interesting aspect of the case is that Lawrence McBride was one of the federal officers who busted them; Lawrence's brother Clarendon McBride had been a Prohibition agent years ago and was involved in the death of two moonshiners.

In January 1933, Schnore and Horner pleaded guilty to the circuit court. Schnore was fined $500 and sentenced to one year in prison. Marvin Horner received one year of prison time as well, but his fine was only $250. Both men were to be paroled immediately on the condition that they pay their fines. Schnore couldn't raise the cash, so he was sent to the penitentiary. Family and friends tried to raise money, but he refused; he didn't want anyone to have to sacrifice for him. His brother even came from Nebraska and offered to pay the fine, but Schnore told him to keep his money—he might need it someday.

THE RETURN OF BEER

On March 22, 1933, President Franklin Roosevelt signed into law the Cullen–Harrison Act, which legalized beer as long as its alcohol content was 3.2 percent or less. Wine was also made legal, as long its alcohol content was also around 3.2 percent. Many thought this Beer Act would quench the thirst of the consumers of hard alcohol.

The Beer Act would be the end of the speakeasy, blind tigers and blind pigs. But what would end wasn't as important as what the bill would bring: revenue from licenses and taxes back into the local governments of Oregon.

On the first day that beer licenses were available, the city collected $8,000 total from four hundred applicants. The demand for beer was high, higher than the local brewers could supply. There were only two breweries set up for the return of beer, one in Pendleton and one in Portland. The Portland Brewery said that when beer became legal on April 7, 1933, the want for it would outpace the speed at which they could brew it; they expected to run out in fifteen minutes.

People were excited for the return of beer, and many people had "New Year's beer" parties scheduled for the evening of April 6. Most of these

Three people enjoying glasses of beer in Clackamas County. *Author's collection.*

145

parties were canceled when it became clear that they wouldn't be able to get any of the legal beer.

The legality of beer did not kill moonshining but did put it on life support. After this, there are only a few more tales of moonshiners during this period. Here is one last story of a novice moonshiner's bad luck.

AN UNLUCKY MOONSHINER IN BEND

An unlucky would-be moonshiner was busted on his first day of 'shining at the end of August 1933, nearly five months after beer became legal. He apparently had quite the elaborate setup built for him. He paid $200 for a fifty-gallon still that included a rectifier. If he had known that in only a few months, hard alcohol would once again be legal, would he have gone to such an effort? The customer base was already short, as many Oregonians switched to the now-legal beer.

C.A. King started his supposed first day of moonshining at seven thirty in the morning. By nine fifteen, the still had caught fire and blew up a pressure tank, the noise of which startled the neighbors, who called the Bend Fire Department. Before the fire department could put out the fire, King's shed was destroyed, and his house was partially scorched. Worse than that, Sheriff Claude McCauley arrived on the scene, arrested King and took his new, destroyed still with him as evidence.

THE END OF PROHIBITION

On December 4, 1933, the Twenty-First Amendment passed, repealing the Eighteenth Amendment. Prohibition was officially over. This, of course, wasn't the end of moonshining—it continues to this day—but it was the end of the "romantic era" of moonshining, that enduring image of outlaws operating secret stills in makeshift dugouts, sheds or even caves or driving through the night in fast cars on dark backroads where the only illumination is from their headlamps and the light that shines down from the moon above.

Moonshining did continue after Prohibition, but to a much smaller degree. This still was busted in Eugene, Oregon in 1934. *Courtesy of the Lane County History Museum.*

Two officers standing next to confiscated moonshining equipment that is strapped to an automobile. *Courtesy of Deschutes County Historical Society.*

Legacy

Moonshine is still alive and well, though, the term has been stretched outside of its origins. In every liquor store, there are bottles of corn whiskey labeled with the word *moonshine*. But that's not true outlaw moonshine. That is commerce trading in on the legacy of outlaws for profit, consumed by people just wanting a taste of outlaw culture. A step past that for someone who wants to dabble in the outlaw lifestyle of making liquor is to buy a small home distilling kit; they are readily available online, marketed as moonshine stills. Type "moonshine still" into any of the popular shopping sites, and low-volume stills can be purchased for less than a couple hundred dollars. The legality of using them is a different story. But maybe the mild risk is part of the thrill? For this author, the way to feel part of the storied outlaw history of moonshiners in Oregon is to be the one to document it.

BIBLIOGRAPHY

Albany (OR) Democrat. "Minors Fined for Larceny and for Having Cigarets." April 16, 1924.

———. "Reckless Driver Is Fined." May 1, 1924.

Albany (OR) Evening Herald. "Funeral for Kendall Will Be Saturday." June 22, 1922.

———. "Healy Was Born Near Scene of Tragic Death." June 22, 1922.

———. "West Slays Linn Sheriff and Pastor." June 22, 1922.

Alumni Directory of the Oregon Agricultural College, Corvallis, Oregon. Corvallis, OR: OAC Alumni Association, 1925.

Bureau of Alcohol, Tobacco, Firearms and Explosives. "Glen H. Price." September 23, 2016. https://www.atf.gov/our-history/fallen-agents/glenn-h-price.

Bend (OR) Bulletin. Ad for *The Last Raid of Sheriff Kendall of Linn County.* July 07, 1923.

———. "County Offers Reward for Dynamiters; Price of $750 Is Placed on Head of Each." March 9, 1926.

———. "Dry Officer Kills Moonshining Suspect in Raid on Booze Plant on High Desert." February 18, 1926.

———. "Life of State Officer Threatened Only Few Days Before Dynamiting." March 8, 1926.

———. "Prohi Officer Shoots Member of Booze Gang." June 11, 1926.

———. "She Escaped Death by Miracle." March 10, 1926.

———. "State Officer Is Exonerated After Killing." February 19, 1926.

———. "Still Explosion Sets Fire Here." August 28, 1933.

———. "Tells Moonshine Tragedy." July 5, 1923.

———. "Vayle Taylor." February 23, 1926.

Bend (OR) Bulletin Extra. "Officer's Home Dynamited." March 8, 1926.

Billings (MT) Gazette. "Pigs Get Soused on Mash; Squeal and Walk Zigzag." March 26, 1920.

Capital Journal (Salem, OR). "Booze Blinds and Paralyzes." April 25, 1929.

———. "Card Row Is Held Reason for Slaying." December 1, 1930.

———. "Continue to Dry Up Legion." September 14, 1932.

———. "50 Days Jail for Owner of Blasted Still." April 21, 1932.

———. "Grand Jury Asks New Bastile for Polk County." October 5, 1922.

———. "Grand Jury to Probe Murder." December 1, 1930.

———. "Indian to Face Second Murder Trial on Jan 15." December 28, 1922.

———. "Not Guilty Says Indian." October 4, 1922.

———. "Trio's Victim Badly Beaten; Arrests Made." January 27, 1932.

———. "The Warren Verdict." October 12, 1922.

Chandler, JD. "Keep Growing Wiser." *Weird Portland* (blog), March 18, 2016. http://weirdportland.blogspot.com/2016/03/keep-growing-wiser.html.

Cooper, Matt, ed. *Oregon Quarterly* 93, no. 3 (2014). University of Oregon.

Corvallis (OR) Gazette-Times. "'Bill' Henderson Kills E.B. Mills." December 1, 1930.

———. "Court Sessions Continue Today with New Cases." September 27, 1932.

———. "E.B. Mills Ad." October 11, 1924.

———. "Garrett Fined." April 24, 1930.

———. "Gets a Heavy Fine." September 22, 1925.

———. "Henderson Plea to Be on Friday." December 3, 1930.

———. "Henderson Said He Had to Shoot." January 7, 1931.

———. "Joe Harkins Is in County Jail." September 26, 1932.

———. "Local Brevities." May 29, 1930.

———. "Local Officers Get Bootleggers." November 19, 1930.

———. "Murder in First Degree Says Jury." December 2, 1930.

———. "Not Guilty, Is Henderson Plea." December 5, 1930.

———. "Only One Year Given Harkins This Morning." September 30, 1932.

Crook County Journal (Prineville, OR). "Moonshining Is Alleged." July 22, 1915.

———. "Not Guilty Is Plea." February 26, 1925.

———. "10 Men Arrested in Liquor Raids." August 11, 1928.

Densley, Lillian Cummins. "Moy Davis." Saints, Sinners and Snake River Secrets, 2006. http://www.snakeriverhistory.com/moydavis.html.

East Oregonian (Pendleton, OR). "Eccentric Miner Dead." March 10, 1904.
———. "Page 4." September 06, 1921.
Eugene Guard. "Alleged Rum Vender Slain at Corvallis." November 30, 1930.
———. "C.C. McBride Has Defender at Bend." June 21, 1926.
———. "Legionnaire Killed." September 14, 1932.
———. "Sutherland Inquest Set Friday." November 26, 1930.
———. "Woman, 77, Bags Deer for 60th Straight Year." October 25, 1957
Eugene Register. "$500 Offered for Killer." August 30, 1930.
———. "Gun Fight Ends 11 Days Hard Search for Killer." November 25, 1930.
———. "Hunt for Slayer Is Continued." September 1, 1930.
Evening Herald. Klamath Falls, OR. "Big Still Seized and Two Arrested." September 1, 1932.
———. "Headquarters of Legion Raided." September 13, 1932.
———. "Man Slain in Liquor Feud at Corvallis." December 1, 1930.
———. "Officer Claims Liquor Killing Was Accidental." February 19, 1926.
———. "Pair Arrested on Liquor Count." February 12, 1932.
Gazette-Times (Corvallis, OR). "Moonshiners Fined and Sent to Jail." December 30, 1915.
Gresham (OR) Outlook. "Nettie Left Indelible Mark on Sandy Area." November 3, 2017.
Hiatt, Isaac. *Thirty-One Years in Baker County.* Baker, OR: Abbott & Foster, 1893.
Holbrook, Stewart. "Elbow Bending for Giants." *Esquire,* April 1954.
Independence (OR) Enterprise. "Page 4." October 13, 1922.
Klamath (OR) News. "Corvallis Restaurant Man Killed." November 30, 1930.
———. "Interesting Motion Picture to Be Shown in Klamath County Towns." August 30, 1924.
La Grande (OR) Observer. "Big Still Taken by Officers in Wallowa County." December 29, 1932.
———. "Schnoor Stays in Pen, Choice." March 14, 1933.
———. "Vile Booze Takes Toll; Boy Passed." March 27, 1925.
Lebanon Express. "School Report." October 13, 1893.
Lincoln County Leader. "Eddyville." September 26, 1919.
Malheur Enterprise. "Booze Makers Locked Up." July 24, 1915
Maupin Times. "Fred Martin Dead." February 4, 1921.
McCarver, M.M. *Laws of a General and Local Nature.* Oregon City, OR: Asahel Bush, Territorial Printer, 1853.
Medford Mail Tribune. "Advent of Legal Beer Spells End for Blind Tigers." April 06, 1933.

———. "Cargo of Liquor Halted on Road." September 11, 1932.

———. "Death in Wake of Corvallis Bootleg Fuss." November 30, 1930.

———. "Depression Hits County Whoopee." January 24, 1932.

———. "Hand Parole Plea Due Ensuing Week." March 14, 1932.

———. "Policemen Swap Car for Liquor Arrest Makers." February 7, 1932.

———. "Still Sets Fire to Salem Home." April 21, 1932.

Miami News-Record. "Spry." January 5, 1958.

Michno, Gregory. *Deadliest Indian War in the West.* Caldwell, ID: Caxton Press, 2007.

Moore, Mark. "Lotus Isle Amusement Park." PdxHistory.com, October 22, 2017. http://www.pdxhistory.com/html/lotus_isle.html.

Morning Oregonian. "Alleged Moonshiners Held." June 29, 1920.

———. "Alleged "Moonshiners" Held in Multnomah County Jail on Charge of Operating in Upper M'Kenzie River County." July 22, 1915.

———. "Arrested Moonshiner." September 10, 1901.

———. "Big Elephant Goes on Rampage, Caught." May 17, 1922.

———. "Big Liquor Haul Made." April 24, 1920.

———. "Bootlegger Learns Cost of Generosity." July 31, 1919.

———. "Both Albany Men Shot from Behind." June 23, 1922.

———. "Capture of Still Closes Long Vigil," June 19, 1918

———. "City Will Be Host to Huge Elephant." December 2, 1931.

———. "Erecting of Still Described at Trial." December 18, 1915.

———. "Fair Board Owner of Huge Elephant." October 6, 1931.

———. "Death Deemed Accident." February 20, 1926.

———. "Dry Agents Slain by Indian." September 4, 1922.

———. "Dry Law Violation Charged." October 30, 1920.

———. "Grape Juice Case Heard." January 5, 1921.

———. "Guise Outwits 2 in Moonshining Raid." July 21, 1915.

———. "Hogs' Tipst [*sic*] Revel Reveals Big Still." March 26, 1920.

———. "Indian Acquitted of Murder Charge." October 13, 1922.

———. "Indictments Are Sought." February 12, 1921.

———. "Japanese Moonshiner Sentenced." May 23, 1917.

———. "Liquor Case Dismissed." October 19, 1922.

———. "Moonshine Inquiry Promises Sensation." May 05, 1920.

———. "Offer Causes Raid." July 19, 1915.

———. "1,500 Bond in Dry Case." October 15, 1920.

———. "Operator of Still Tells All in Court." January 25, 1921.

———. "Outlaw Sutherland Shot Dead by Posse." November 26, 1930.

———. "Permit Refused Again." June 7, 1923.

———. "Portland May Have Biggest Elephant in Captivity." May 20, 1931.

———. "Prisoner's Friend Held for Threats." January 21, 1921.

———. "Rearrangement of the Service Asked for in Baker County." November 25, 1901.

———. "Rum Possession Brings Redskin 60-Day Sentence." September 9, 1937.

———. "Sake Still Found." March 30, 1917.

———. "Seeley-Connett Marriage." November 1, 1909.

———. "Sunday Raids Net Ten Chinese." October 12, 1914

———. "Three Admit Liquor Selling." November 13, 1917.

———. "Three Members of One Family Fined for Bootlegging." July 31, 1919.

———. "Tusko Crumbles Walls of Abode." December 16, 1931.

———. "Underground Still Found by Sheriff." September 2, 1920.

———. "Whiskey Maker Surprised." May 9, 1919.

———. "Whisky Owner Sentenced." January 22, 1936.

———. "Witnesses Recall Grand Ronde Fray." October 11, 1922.

———. "Woman Arrested Again." April 5, 1920.

———. "Woman Held as Moonshiner." November 15, 1919.

———. "Wood Hides Liquor Cache." January 6, 1920.

———. "Woman Is Convicted." December 3, 1920.

———. "Woman Wields Knife as Deputy Arrests Her for Bootlegging." May 8, 1919.

Morning Register. "Still Is Found in Cave." September 2, 1920.

National Register of Historic Places. "OMB NO.1024-0018." July 25, 2000.

Newberg Graphic. "Big Moonshine Still Is Raided." August 5, 1920.

Oregon City Courier. "Bootleggers Are Caught This Week." January 2, 1919.

———. "Erickson Stages Wild West Show." May 10, 1917.

Oregon City Enterprise. "Federal Jury Finds Mrs. Connett Guilty on Three Counts." April 2, 1920.

———. "Moonshine Is Found at Milwaukie Farm of Three Austrians." October 22, 1920.

———. "Moonshiner Must Serve Six Months in Federal Prison." May 20, 1921.

———. "Two Stills Are Found by Sheriff in County." November 14, 1919.

Oregon Daily Journal. "Citizens of Maupin Suspecting Poison, Want Body Exhumed." February 5, 1921.

———. "Erickson Property Will Be Divided." September 9, 1917.

———. "Erickson Tavern Property Bought for Summer Home." June 5, 1919.

———. "Ex-Saloon Man Ordered to Jail Can't Pay Fine." August 19, 1920.

———. "Flegel Believes Basich Was Head of Newberg Still." October 14, 1920.

———. "Fugitive Moonshiner Is Caught in Idaho" July 23, 1918.

———. "Here and Hereafter." May 27, 1931.

———. "Hotels." December 22, 1908.

———. "Husband and Wife Arrested; Police Find Much Booze." November 15, 1922.

———. "Impressions and Observations of the Journal Man." March 12, 1920.

———. "Impressions and Observations of the Journal Man." March 13, 1920.

———. "Impressions and Observations of the Journal Man." March 14, 1920.

———. "Impressions and Observations of the Journal Man." March 15, 1920.

———. "Impressions and Observations of the Journal Man." December 5, 1921.

———. "Jarrell Yet Free." June 20, 1918.

———. "Keg of Whiskey Placed in Evidence." December 19, 1915.

———. "Linn County Sheriff and Pastor Slain." June 22, 1922.

———. "Lotus Isle Gets Giant Elephant." May 25, 1931.

———. "Moonshiners from Lane County Fined and Sent to Prison" December 27, 1915.

———. "Moonshine Makes 3 Widows. Lockley Describes Scene." June 22, 1922.

———. "No Arrests Made by Police for a Ten Hour Period." January 6, 1916.

———. "Page 10." September 22, 1921.

———. "Prisoner Taken by Til Taylor Contributes $5." August 20, 1920.

———. "Prohi Director Says Bootleg is Rankest Poison." May 2, 1920.

———. "Revenue Men Rushed in Where Bad Luck Feared to Put Its Foot." March 26, 1920.

———. "Seven Big Barrels of Wine and Much Alcohol Unearthed." February 21, 1921.

———. "Still Operators Plead Guilty and Are Fined." July 2, 1918.

———. "Store Is So Popular Police Investigate; Moonshine Is Found." January 23, 1921.

———. "Ton of Headache Tortures Tusko." December 6, 1931.

———. "Wood Alcohol So Far Skips City." December 27, 1919.

Oregon Native Son. Portland, OR: Native Son, 1900.

Oregon Statesman (Salem, OR). "Bomb Planted for Dry Agent." March 9, 1926.

———. "Bomb Plot Purse Asked." March 11, 1926.

———. "Kaboris Death Starts Inquiry." June 12, 1926.

———. "Large Moonshine Still Taken Near McKenzie." September 23, 1923.

———. "Liquor Dealer Dies in Battle with Officers." June 11, 1926.

———. "McBride Is Exonerated of Blame by Coroner's Jury." June 13, 1926.

———. "Page 1." March 10, 1926.

———. "Posse Shoots Sutherland in Lair in Woods." November 26, 1930.

———. "Sutherland Clue Is Supplied by Portland Barber." September 9, 1930.

———. "Warren Trail Is in Tangle." October 11, 1922.

Oregon Sunday Journal (Portland, OR). "Slayer's Widow Relates Circumstances about Linn County Tragedy." June 25, 1922.

Robertson, Wyndham. *Oregon; Our Right and Title*. WA: J. & G.S. Gideon, 1846.

Roseburg (OR) News-Review. "Moonshine Quality Is Getting Better, Dry Agent Asserts." August 15, 1922.

Sandy (OR) Post. "Connett: Queen of the Moonshiners." October 22, 2014.

———. "Community Remembers One-of-A-Kind Woman." October 22, 2014.

———. "1964: Sandy's Renowned Nettie Connett Dies at 84." October 22, 2014.

Schepps, Michael. "Erickson's Saloon." Oregon Encyclopedia, last updated September 6, 2022. https://www.oregonencyclopedia.org/articles/ericksons-saloon/.

Spokesman-Review (Spokane, WA). "Find Still Under Ground." September 2, 1920.

Statesman Journal (Salem, OR). "Explosion of Still Sets House Ablaze; Tenant Is Arrested." April 21, 1932.

———. "Prohibition Agents Foxy." January 28, 1923.

———. "Tales of Rum Pedlar Differ." April 26, 1929.

Sunday Oregonian (Portland, OR). "Fate of Ray Sutherland Remains Mystery." November 9, 1930.

———. "Liquor Trial Is Set." January 16, 1921.

———. "Moonshine Plant Raided." September 12, 1920.

———. "Moonshining for 5 Years Laid to 2." July 18, 1915.

———. "Oregon Moonshiners." October 8, 1911.

———. "Section 3, Page 6." May 26, 1912.

———. "Still Raid Tax $7,900." August 15, 1920.

————. "Tusko Held Mistreated." May 31, 1931.

United States Congress House Committee on the Judiciary. *Hearings Before the Committee on the Judiciary House of Representatives, Seventy-First Congress, Second Session* […]. Washington, D.C.: United States Printing Office, 1930.

Wood, Dick. "King Killer of the Mountain." *Crime Does Not Pay* 1, no. 39 (May 1945).

World. "Pioneer Saloon Keeper Is Dead." January 3, 1925.

ABOUT THE AUTHOR

Photo by Rachel Rogers.

Bruce Haney has been referred to as the town historian for Boring, Oregon. He runs a history group called Boring Oregon History, gives monthly history speeches and is the author of *Eccentric Tales of Boring, Oregon*.

Outside of Boring, Bruce likes to pass the time by finding something he is interested in and then learning everything he can about it. Sometimes it leads to a book like the one you are currently reading, or sometimes he just learns all there is to know about an obscure punk rock band or some old, trashy but fun movie.